Dearest

MW00944602

of your support. I couldn't ask for a better sister-in-law. May Gods light continue to shine in all you do. May He continue to keep you healthy.

Love
Norma Jean

1

# '514'

## South Harris Avenue

Book Three of
**The Tin Train Series**

By Norma Jean

Copyright
Text Copyright 2013
Norma Jean (Baas) Denty
All Rights Reserved

Denty Publications
dentypublications.com

# Contents

# Preface

I have been working on this series most of my life.

I have been praying to God to guide me every step of the way. Only He can make sense of what is in my heart.

My Pastor kept telling us all in God's timing, not ours. We must have patience.

I talk a lot in my books about the Christmas village and the Christmas train. I talk about how dad was at Christmas time.

I have our Christmas train and Christmas village from when we were kids. The tracks are no more. The train I have only three cars. The village is for the most part still intact. There are a few missing outer shells of the village. It is made of wood and has an outer layer that is colored individually to personalize each piece.

The icing on the cake was the Christmas of 2012. I put these pieces around my Christmas tree just like when we were kids. My husband even made me a table to make my set up just like when I was a kid. I place the cardboard chimney around my tree as well. I love lots of tinsel just as my dad did. I love the way it sparkles when the lights hit it just so.

It is beautiful.

The Christmas of 2012, I looked at all of these village pieces. One of houses says railroad; one says supermarket; one says courthouse.

The piece that really struck me was the school's name. My childhood village school's name is Lincoln School. I live in Lincoln Village North, and I work for Prairie Lincoln Elementary. This was the final sign to me from God that it is time for me to finish these books.

Thank you, God for helping me.

# Dedication

I dedicate this book to my whole family. You all have supported me no matter what I started. This not only includes all my brothers and sisters but all the nieces and nephews and all the great nieces and great nephews.

May God continue to bless our family in all of our endeavors.

You supported me when I wanted Christmas in July. You supported me when we had Christmas in December. You supported me through all my many endeavors.

May I again say thank you.

I pray that God bless all of you. I pray God bless all the future generations of our family. I pray He keeps them all from the evils of this world. I pray that our grandchildren (mine included) keep on the straight path of God's grace and goodness.

Thanks so much for your support through the years. May God continue to keep us healthy and strong in the faith.

## Acknowledgments

First off, I want to thank God for letting me have all these memories to write about. Without God in my life, I would have gone on a completely different path. I doubt it would have been a good path.

Thanks to all those people who knew our family and helped us out whenever you could.

Thanks to all my brothers and sisters who, I hope, love me still in spite of all these revelations. Thank you so much.

I want to thank my daughter for being the amazing, beautiful woman you are today. No words can describe how much I admire you as a woman. I will love you forever.

To all the nieces and nephews out there who love us as parents, aunts, and uncles, in spite of all of our shortcomings, a great big thank you as well. Thank you for putting up with all of those times you had to sit and listen to us reminisce about our childhood. Thank you, all of you for your patience. Thank you for loving your parents, your aunts, and your uncles in spite of your childhood.

I love all of you as well.

May God continue to allow us to grow as a family! May he embrace each and every one of us with the hugs only He can give!

I want to thank amazon.com for helping to make all this possible. Amazon connected us with create space to do the printing. This has really helped in putting all this together.

Thanks to my husband (Jeff) who read several books to learn the process to get us where we are today. Thank you so much for all your hard work. There are no words to describe how I feel. I hope you know. I am telling the world so that you know how much it means to me. I love you.

## The Brownie Camera

Vera was the oldest girl in the family. She was also the artist. She was the one who played the violin to the envy of all. She was allowed to do things none of the rest of us ever got to do.

Vera was allowed to go to the Columbus symphony orchestra when they performed. She was an usher. Through the ushering program, she got to go to hear the music. I thought this was great. It was an opportunity to mingle with other musicians.

One of the special things Vera did was the usage of a Brownie camera.

One bright and sunny day after Grandma had come to stay Vera got into one of her creative modes. She decided to take pictures of everyone. She even took pictures of grandma. Grandma was livid. Grandma hated to have her picture taken. Pictures were really expensive. I think this is the real reason grandma was mad. She was madder than a hornet.

But some of the few pictures we have of us are the ones Vera would sneak and take. I think this is pretty special. If I have never said it before Vera I will say it now for all to see. Thank you for taking all those pictures with that Brownie camera.

## Dad Has A Girlfriend

Just a few day before my dad's girlfriend had her fifth baby we all went to the bean dinner at Westgate Park. Grandma usually took us. But dad took us this time.

It was always so much fun. It usually took place around 4th of July. They served bean soup. It was always good and inexpensive. They always had rides and all kinds of contests for the kids to enter. They had cracker eating contests, sack races, ponytail contests, and my favorite the twisting contest. My brothers usually won the sack race.

The girlfriend and her kids came along this year. Dad had never had a girlfriend since our mother died. That is why all of us went to the bean dinner this year.. He had not been drinking much either trying to impress her. I thought it was great.

This year everyone went because dad was trying to impress his new girl-friend. Debbie won the cracker-eating contest this year. Once you eat the allotted amount of crackers you had to whistle to let those in charge know you were done. Fred won the watermelon contest. I won the ponytail and the twisting contest. If you won, you got one silver dollar for third place, three silver dollars for second place, and five silver dollars for first place. I earned eight silver dollars. Debbie earned a total of five. Freddie won five. Larry won a total of five for the sack races. Larry always won the wheel barrel races. We were not too surprised. When Larry was not winning the sack races, Jimmy was winning the sack races. Jimmy and Larry teamed up this year, won the wheel barrel contest, and split the money. They fought back and forth as to who would win. It was so much fun. The bean soup was unusually good this year. We had a lot of money to spend. Larry saved his like he always did. Jimmy usually saved his too.

Dad wanted all of us to get to know his girlfriend. Dad insisted we get to know her. When dad insisted you did it without questioning. I did not realize he was trying to impress her. While we were sitting here with the girlfriend, it was strained at first. What do you say to an adult you do not know?

I remember sitting around the picnic table in the shade resting for a little while. Dad had taken his girlfriend's kids and his younger ones for a few rides. A few of us older ones were sitting with his girlfriend. I wasn't that old, I was ten years old. We all just started talking about things like the weather and how much fun we were having today.

Then the girlfriend asked, "How did Jimmy get hurt." She wanted us to believe she did not know about it. Jim was only six years old. He had done something that an older sister and brother had done. He had heard the story many times and he thought he would try it. It sounded like fun. Dad thought it was neat when the older siblings did it. He bragged about it all the time. Dad would throw back his head, laugh, and say how funny he thought it was.

He would say, "Because Fred and Debbie had missed me so much they rode their tricycle down to see me at the garage."

This question from the girlfriend who was not a family member wanting to know family secrets. Well we just looked at each other at first. We did not say a thing.

Then I said, "Dad whipped him for doing something he was not supposed to do." The girlfriend was very shocked. I said, "Jim was only following in the footsteps of an older brother and sister. Our father told the story to him and all of us with relish. Jimmy, like his older brother and sister, just wanted to see his dad. He missed him. He only did what they had done. Dad helped them earn some money. Jimmy wanted to earn some money too. No one else received a whipping. But Jim did." Jim was black and blue all over every inch of his body.

He had bruises all over his face. He had a black eye. This punishment did not fit the crime. He only did what his older brother and sister had done. They did not get as much as a reprimand. The punishment did not fit the crime. Then I told the girlfriend, "That was not the end of the punishment. Dad proceeded to pull down Jim's pants and sit him on a hot radiator, and his butt was blistered something horrible the blisters turned black," at this point she gasped, she couldn't believe what she was hearing. I did not know she was such a good actress.

The girlfriend said, "If I was your mother and your dad and I were married he would not ever raise a hand to another one of you children. I would personally see to it."

I was skeptical, never in our entire lives with the exception of our mother had another adult even thought of interceding where our dad was concerned. Here was a virtual stranger trying to make us believe she would do it.

I did not know at the time that she was there when dad beat Jimmy. She was egging our dad on, the whole time. Jimmy had not told me any of this. I do not trust easy. It was hard for me to believe she would stand up for us. No! I did not trust her any more than I did any other adult. I wanted to give her the benefit of the doubt. I wanted to believe.

Later on, much, much later on, I learned she was snickering and egging our dad on.

The day of Jimmy's beating; the girlfriend was actually at the garage.

## Ten Year Old Baby Sitter

Before my dad's girlfriend went into the hospital to have her baby. (This was baby number five for her, my dad had eleven). We did a lot of babysitting for her kids that summer. When she did go into the hospital, she had left her four kids at home alone. Her oldest child was only six years old. He was watching them. She told my dad her kids were alone; she also told him that children's services was snooping around. If they saw that a virtual baby was watching her kids, she would have lost all of her kids immediately.

Dad went immediately to get her kids and bring them to our house. He took Karen with him. Karen said what she had seen and smelled at this house made her deathly ill. She said, "The kids were filthy; the house was a wreck; the house smelled of urine; there wasn't any food anywhere in the house to be found." Karen said, "She did not know what they had been eating but it was all gone." She packed up a few articles of clothing for each of the kids. She also packed whatever else she thought they would need. Karen was quite responsible for her age soon to be seventeen. She had been helping Grandma out a lot over the past few years.

When the girlfriend came home from the hospital dad told me to go with her to help. He felt she had too much to do by herself. It was only a couple of days before she was back in the hospital. She had developed another complication. So all of her kids and me included were loaded up into a car and brought back to our house, again. She was not in the hospital long this time. A few days later, we were back at her house.

That summer at the age of ten, I began my duties as chief cook and bottle washer. It was not even for my own brothers and sisters. I got up fed them their breakfast; sterilized the baby bottles; cleaned the house from top to bottom; kept the kids clean; fed them their lunch; washed clothes; washed the dishes; played with the kids; fed them their supper; and gave them their baths; and got them ready for bed. Last and not least of all, I catered to the girlfriend's every needs. She asked me to get her something even if I was sitting and relaxing myself I got up and fetched it.

Dad had taught us well, I was a genuine work alcoholic. I catered to dad's girlfriend but it was fun because she and dad felt I was responsible enough to do all these things. I felt important for a change. I was not just the middle kid with no one to play with. She even talked to me, which Grandma certainly never did. At home, Karen got all the credit for doing everything. Even I thought Karen did everything. If she did, how was this possible for me to know how to do so much?

However, the days dragged on into weeks and even a month passed. It was no longer fun. I was doing everything by myself.

At home at least when I did all these things I had help. Here there was no one to help. I yearned for the help of my brothers and sisters. I yearned for their support. I had never been away from home so long.

The girlfriend was gone most of the time again by now she was feeling her old self. There was no longer any reason to keep me here. She was capable of handling her own kids again. She started going back to my dad's garage. Here I was stuck babysitting for a woman I did not know and for kids I did not know. I did not get any pay for all this work either. Her kids started not listening to me. Her oldest did not like it that I had taken his job away from him.

I was homesick.

I had been here a month and a half and I wanted to go home. I felt I was there just being used as a workhorse. There was not a phone, so calling home was out of the question. Finally, after seven weeks with no end in sight and I was throwing all kinds of hints that I wanted to go see my family. She said, "Well if it means that much to you we will go to see them. Heaven knows why you would want to go see that brood again. It is beyond me."

I was hurt. I was here out of the kindness of my dad's heart working for this woman and she has to say things like this about my family. I did not say anything. They taught us to respect our elders. Then she said, "better yet we will just take you home right now, instead of just visiting." She said, "I was planning upon taking you to the state fair with me next week, but seeing as how your family means more to you then we do, we'll just take you home instead. The state fair was to be your payment for helping out all summer like you did." Again, I was crushed heck we hardly ever got to go any place as grand as the state fair.

I never received a dime. Helping out, was not the word I would use. I did everything. She either sat and watched and supervised or was gone. I did not say a word. If she had asked me to stay to go to the fair with them, I might have. I wanted to scream, holler, and tell her I would stay another whole week just to get a chance to go to the fair. I did not. My earlier childhood upbringing made sure that if I ever wanted anything; I could not do or say anything. The words just would not come.

Now, as an adult looking back, it should have been a warning that she was not to be trusted or loved. Kids always strive to please. They want to think most people mean them no harm, until it is too late. By the time I did get home that summer, I was dejected. So dejected I could not talk to anyone about it. I should have been happy to be home but I hated myself because I felt I had done something wrong by being homesick. It was my punishment, not to go to the fair. Since I could not talk to anyone about it, the things troubling me just kept getting worse.

School started shortly after I got back home. I was in sixth grade and I was in a split class, fifth and sixth grade together. Slowly I started going downhill. I went from A's and B's to B's and C's in just a few short weeks, no one noticed and no one cared. It was a subtle change.

Shortly after school started, dad moved his girlfriend into the upstairs apartment next door. We also owned the house next door. My dad had converted it into two apartments, one up, and one down.

They got married in early October. The girlfriend had asked the pastor of our church to do the ceremony. The pastor already knew a lot of the turmoil we had been through with our dad. He refused to officiate at their wedding. He did not feel they were right for each other. The step-mother to be was furious. She felt it as an affront to her. They got someone else to do the ceremony.

It was neat for a while. We moved into the big house next door, 514. It was now a two-story dwelling again. This done we moved from a two-bedroom house for eleven to an eight-bedroom house for seventeen. Fortunately, one of my older brothers and one of my older sisters had moved out already.

Like it was all summer, the new stepmother spent all her time at the garage. As soon as Karen or I got home from school, she took off to go to the garage. Karen and I proceeded to cook supper. We cleaned the house. We got the kids ready for bed and in bed before she got home. It kept us busy full time, as well as going to school.

Our morning started early too. We got up at five thirty in the morning. We cooked breakfast for all the kids and packed their lunches. We got everyone up and off to school. I was ten and a half and in sixth grade. Karen had just turned sixteen.

One morning Karen and I were late in getting up. The stepmother came running up the step as fast as she could. She screamed as loud as she possibly could. She started shaking us and shaking us she said, "If you are ever late in getting up again, you will wish you hadn't been." Both of us were slapped as well. She pulled us by our hair all the way down the steps.

I continued to go downhill, this was too much for a ten year old to handle. I had never been so scared in all my life. I think all my younger brothers and sisters felt as I did. Again we did not talk about it much. We were not supposed to talk about anything.

Not even so much as a whisper were we allowed to utter.

## No longer Little Boy Blue

The stepmother knew one of grandma's favorites was Daryl. It was only natural since he was only nine months old when our mother died. He was the last of her children and the baby. The sun rose and set with Daryl, as far as grandma was concerned. Daryl could do no wrong. When grandma was around, she thought he was an angel. He really was a sweet child. Perhaps a little spoiled. He not only had grandma to spoil him but ten brothers and sisters as well.

He at a very early age loved music. Grandma especially loved this about him. He started picking out pieces by hearing them on the radio. He could hear it then go play it on the piano or guitar, very gifted. This he could do before the age of five. Grandma started teaching him the notes on the piano. She would show him the keys on the piano. Then she would show him that each key was a note. She showed him he could read the notes off a sheet of music. He could play it this way; he was very fascinated by all of it.

By the time, the stepmother came along Daryl was only four years old. So grandma had to give up her pride and joy that is what Daryl was to her. She felt he was more her son than anyone else's. She had been there for him. If he got sick, she was there. If he had troubles, she was there. Daryl was as much devoted to grandma as she was to him. Grandma's pet nickname for Daryl was little boy blue because he had the prettiest blue eyes. They would sparkle every time he smiled. Even though Daryl called her grandma, she was the only mother he had ever known.

Just like that, when the stepmother came along grandma had to go away from him. How devastating it was for him to lose her. Grandma too was very upset over this.

After this, Daryl started losing touch with reality. He would stare off into space, remembering better times. He started talking to himself.

He was left handed, had always been left handed. The stepmother started getting on his case immediately about this. She said, "You will use your right hand and make no messes either." If at any point, he forgot and used his left hand, she smacked him. The new step-mother was five foot five inches tall. She weighed one-hundred and sixty pound. While she stood over him, she shouted at the top of her lungs. "If I've told you once, I've told you a hundred times to use your right hand." She would proceed to grab whatever he was doing with his left hand and make him use his right hand. It is hard to break a habit like this especially after five years. Eventually he learned but for him the humiliation, the frustration, and the hurt he went through were very traumatic and needless on the stepmother's part. He went from being sunshine and little boy blue to dirt in just a matter of days.

The stepmother's kids were ages six, five, four, and eighteen months and the baby was about four months old. Naturally, Daryl played a lot with her kids because he too was four.

One day while they were playing her youngest boy got hurt. He was the eighteen-month-old baby. He was crying.

So all the rest of her kids said, "Daryl did it, Daryl did it." My dad saw red. Daryl was standing at the top of the basement stairs at the time. Dad backhanded him. Daryl went flying down the flight of stairs his head and mouth hit the concrete floor. His whole mouth was a bloody mass; his permanent teeth were loose, wiggly, and bleeding. Neither the stepmother nor dad went to see Daryl. I went to see him, to cuddle him and to make sure he was okay. I tried to make sure he stayed awake just in case of a concussion, I knew at least that much, I was only ten.

My heart was aching for him. Before dad found out any of the pertinent details of what was going on, all dad could think of was the stepmother's kids said, "Daryl had hurt one of her kids." Daryl was hurt really bad. The eighteen month old was not hurt that bad. It definitely did not merit doing to Daryl what dad had done. Besides when kids, are playing with each other, one is usually going to get hurt, especially if one is only eighteen months old and playing with older children. From that day forward, it was the beginning of a new era for Daryl.

We all tried to protect him as much as we could but we too were only children.

The stepmother's kids found out they could blame Daryl for everything that went wrong and they could get off scott free. They did it quite frequently. Whenever something happened like one of her kids getting hurt or something getting broken they all chimed in unison, "Daryl did it, Daryl did it." She hated that grandma loved Daryl so much. (Of course, I learned all this much later on.) At any point she could make Daryl feel little or helpless or unloved she did it with relish.

Another time Daryl got into trouble was when he was mad at me for something. He hit me in the head with a pop-bottle. My nose was bleeding and it swelled up the size of a golf ball. My nose, my eyes and the whole side of my face was black and blue for three weeks. Daryl was sorry afterwards. He even said he was sorry as soon as he had done it. Ouch! It did hurt, I cried. Daryl cried too, he was so sorry.

The stepmother was not home at the time. When she did get home her kids said, "Daryl did it," before I even got a chance to say it was an accident. Daryl got a bad whipping. I felt like it was my fault. Grandma did not help any; she had been there at the time and said as much, which made me feel even worse.

It took her a long time to get over Daryl getting the whipping. I knew he did not deserve what he had gotten but I did not know what to do or how to stop her from whipping him. We were more protective of him after this episode.

After she whipped him as much and as hard as she did, I kept thinking of the promises she had made at Westgate Park this past summer. The promises she had made at the bean dinner. Her promises were about not whipping us or not letting dad whip us kids again. Here she was doing it instead.

## Wet Mattresses

We found out early how things were going to be. The stepmother's two oldest girls wet the bed every single night. Oh! I can still smell the stench today. If I think of it hard enough, it is one of those smells that would permeate the very air. The urine on the girls and the mattress smelled so bad one would think they had saved it up all day and urinated only on the mattress. They never even tried to clean themselves up afterward. They even went to school smelling of urine. They continued to sleep in that mess the whole night through.

Debbie and Joan got the blame. The stepmother said, "My girls have never wet the bed a single day in their life." We knew this to be false because when we brought her kids to our house earlier in the summer their house smelled of urine. Well the stepmother made Joan and Debbie (as little as they were) carry this double sized heavy spring mattress, outside by themselves. They carried it through two rooms down a flight of stairs and out to the back porch to air and dry.

She did not have a plastic sheet cover over the mattress, just a set of sheets, and a blanket. One days' worth of urine was from these two little girls was enough to make a person gag. A whole weeks' worth was enough to blind a person from the strong odor. Karen and I both told the stepmother, "Joan and Debbie have never wet the bed. Why would they start now?" She said, "They didn't wet their beds they got up in the middle of the night and peed on my daughters' beds." We were furious by this time. She did not know what she was talking about. Why would Debbie and Joan do such a horrible, mean nasty thing to anyone let alone their stepsisters. We let it slide this one time.

The second time, we stood in a force and refused to let Debbie and Joan take one-step to taking that mattress outside. Joan and Debbie were afraid they were going to get a whipping. We told them if we stood together on this, she could not whip all of us at once.

Both grandma and dad had already beaten us. She was not going to beat us down too. Not if we could stop it right from the beginning as a unit.

This time the stepmother saw none of us was going to budge. We told her, "If you want that mattress outside either you do it yourself or your girls are going to do it." We said, "Joan and Debbie did not wet their bed or anyone else's bed. Nor did they climb on top of your girls and urinate on them." We refused to let them take it. We said, "Your daughters have always wet their own beds. We know because we were at your house during the summer. We could smell it on them and on their bedding." With that she knew she was licked she also knew we were not going to budge.

We finally said, "You cannot whip all of us at once and if you even try someone will be on top of you." We told her also, "Debbie and Joan would not dream of getting up in the middle of the night to wet on someone else." We thought that was the most disgusting thought that anyone could say. I think for the first time the stepmother was actually afraid of us.

It was at this time she started new tactics. She did make her daughters carry out the mattress. That weekend she bought a plastic mattress cover.

This is when she started conniving pitting one of us against the other. She actually set us up so that it was her kids against us kids. Saying things like, so and so said that you did this, so and so said that you did that. She started making up lies to get us mad at each other so that we would not stand together against her again.

Sometimes it worked. Once we figured it out though what she was doing, pitting each one of us against the other, it did not work.

Her daughters continued over the years to wet the bed and as usual, their smelly, wet underwear went down to the basement. They went to school smelling of urine. Their mother never stopped them from going that way. We tried to stop them because we were embarrassed for them as well as for ourselves, but they never bothered to listen. They said, "Well it doesn't bother mom so why should it bother you." We had no further arguments to use.

It did not take the stepmother long after the mattress scene to get the measure of each one of us kids. What our weaknesses were and what our strong points were.

## Grandma Kicked Out

Grandma had been raising us.

The stepmother hated it that we still would go to grandma to see how things were supposed to be done. We had been doing it this way for so long it was hard to change a habit.

By this point too, the new stepmother and grandma had, had a falling out. She said, "I refuse to live in the same house with the mother of your dead wife, Arthur. Get her out of here immediately. I will not live in the shadow of Ella."

With this grandma said, "That suits me just fine because I refuse to stay in a house with an upstart gold digger like you." Grandma moved out lock stock and baggage. The only things that grandma took with her were the few personal items that had once been my mother's (including my mother's childhood scrapbook) and her clothes.

Luckily, grandma had invested in a house a long time ago. She had just been renting it out; over the years she had been with us. All of us kids were devastated. Grandma had been a strong hold for us. Yes! She too had a penchant that also bordered on meanness, but she was still our grandma. She was a figurehead of our own dead mother. Now looking back, I think that is exactly why the stepmother got rid of her. She did not want us to remember our mother. Grandma was just a reminder of the past.

Yes! We had our differences with grandma but we had come to terms with them and had come to know a peace of sorts.

{*One thing different between Grandma and the stepmother was Grandma always said, "Do your work like you enjoy it. Try the easiest way of doing everything so that you get it done in half the time. This gives you more time to enjoy yourself and enjoy life." Looking back now it was a great motto and I still use it today.*}

Yes! It sounds selfish but that is what she taught us, to go with an attitude that you love everything. It will all go so much more smoothly. We tried to and it did seem to help.

The stepmother saw these things in us and she did not like us to enjoy ourselves. Yes in the beginning, we did not think of things as work. We thought everything was fun and we helped each other out by pitching in.

{*Writing this story is a healing of sorts. It reminds me of some of the good times with grandma. Thanks grandma for telling us to enjoy what we do.*}

The stepmother tried to reteach us. She said, "Do not enjoy your work. Work was to be a punishment." For me I was too old to listen. It was hard for me to retrain myself. I liked grandma's idea about work. To an outsider who did not truly understand why we acted as if we enjoyed everything. It would seem like we were always joking around. We were just trying to make an impossible task seem better. It would also seem to an outsider that we were doing it deliberately. We were trying to get out of work, when this was the actual way we were taught to enjoy doing our work.

Grandma would say, "There will be a lot of things that you will disagree with out there. If you can make the smaller task seem easier and make everything a game, life will be tolerable."

To the stepmother however, it seemed that we thought all of life was one big game. She could not stand anyone who enjoyed himself or herself. She tried valiantly to reteach our way of thinking and tried to turn our lives around. All I could do was stand by, watch, and listen.

I loved grandma's way of thinking. I did not think that I could ever go back to thinking that I could not enjoy something. For my younger brothers and sisters were not so lucky. The stepmother threatened a beating at every turn. She constantly would say, "Think this is a game," SMACK! "Do you think it is funny," SMACK! All I could do was to stand and watch. There was not a thing I could do. I got my own fair share of smacks. No one was exempt from this treatment. We were all treated the same. Inside however I did do the things with a smile, without anyone knowing, inside my head. No one could take away my thoughts.

I knew I would never survive this new turmoil we were going through, if I did not enjoy what I was doing.

The stepmother hit us at every turn. We would be humming and singing and she would slap us in the head or smack us on the side of the face. She would say, "That will be enough of that."

Thanks to grandma, her training helped us to tolerate some of our latest treatment. We just did not know it at the time.

Junior got married and moved out. He still worked for our dad. Dad still refused to pay him. Junior's wife put a stop to it. I cannot blame her. She said to Junior, "You now have a family of your own to support. You need to get a job that will pay you a salary. You will not let your dad take your money all the time." This was a pretty hard concept for Junior. He had always taken this treatment from dad.

Vera was forced out of the house, as well. The stepmother refused to let her stay. The stepmother felt if you had graduated from High School, you were out the door and on your own. She felt you needed to get a job and be on your own.

## Christmas with the Stepmother

Christmas was here. Dad was always very excited about Christmas. This year seems to be no different he was again in his element. The stepmother and dad went shopping together. They wanted to buy all of us something special. I think they were trying to impress us kids with how much they were going to do for us.

Christmas Eve she was ranting and raving all night long, so that no one else got any sleep. She figured that if she was going to lose sleep so was everyone else. She kept screaming, "About how the floors needed swept, and mopped and all the furniture needed dusting." She said, "I have all these pies to bake." She said, "I have already been making cookies, candy, and fruitcake since Thanksgiving." She said, "I am sick and tired of it all. She was tired of having to work like a dog and for what, no thanks." She said, "You brats are nothing but a bunch of good for nothing lazy asses and she was tired of putting up with it all."

She had all Dads' family coming and the house was a pigsty.

It was not the same this Christmas. Dad liked doing everything Christmas Eve. It was the tradition his parents brought from Germany. The stepmother did not like decorating on Christmas Eve. All she did that Christmas was gripe and complain about how she had to wrap all these presents all by herself. She hated decorating the tree. She especially did not like the fact that we had special traditions and she did not want them to continue. She put up all the decorations and thought somebody else should have done it. She said, "I refuse to put anything up that once belonged to her" (meaning our mother.)

A whole many other things that could have gone wrong that Christmas went wrong. She hated not being able to go to bed until the wee hours of the morning. She would not even let dad do the usual Christmas Eve unwrap. We had to wait until she got a decent amount of rest. We had to keep all the little ones quiet until such a time had come.

She (the stepmother) spoiled the one season dad really loved. It was never the same as it was before.

All Christmas morning, even after she did get up all she did was complain. She was literally in a bad mood all day long. This set the mood for everyone else. It was never the same on Christmas after she came along. Christmas was supposed to be a time of rejoicing and having fun with the family. She was literally destroying the traditions that we had followed closely for many years.

She did not want to have to cook the big traditional turkey dinner either. She was tired of all the festivities. She was tired of working like a dog for all her ungrateful stepchildren. She was sick and tired of everything that had to do with Christmas. Karen and I cooked the meal this year.

We did not set up the Christmas train this year. We did not put up our Christmas village this year either. Dad was not very happy about it but he did not say anything either. Dad just wanted to make her happy. It was her first year in the family he thought we should just let her do what she wanted. He just wanted to make her happy.

Dad wanted more tinsel. The stepmother did not. Dad wanted the village set up on the table he had made years ago. She did not. So on and on they fought. It seemed like it lasted the whole last half of the month of December. Arguing! Arguing! And more arguing!!

This year I got a showboat. I used to write plays. I would make up these plays and have my little brothers, and sisters act them out. My little brothers and sisters enjoyed helping me. I was the narrator. We did one for Christmas this year. The parents thought it would be neat to get me a showboat. We always had fun doing the performances. It was neat. Just like a real showboat. It had a real stage with cardboard people, with plastic stands, great props that would slide up and down. My younger brothers and sisters loved listening to my stories and helping with the stage performances.

Christmas came and went and we were back in school.

## Joan Bathing the Children

Another thing that I started to hate this past summer and fall was, Joan my littlest sister had to wash the hair of both stepsisters'. Whenever they needed, their hair washed Joan had to do it. The oldest step sister was six years old. She had curly unruly hair. Once Joan washed the hair, she had to comb and brush it out too. If you have ever had to comb out or brush out curly hair, you can understand what is happening. Curly hair is kinky. As soon as you comb it out it is a tangled up mess. It is unruly. For Joan to have to do this while she herself was so young was too much, I thought it was too much to expect.

Then the next oldest was five. She was a little bit bigger than Joan was too. She like her sister had curly hair. Joan was small for her age. Joan was the same age as the oldest one and smaller then both of the stepmother's daughters. Joan had to wash, rinse, comb, and roll their hair in rollers even though they had naturally curly hair. I could not tell the justification there was to rolling their hair in curlers especially when they had curly hair.

Karen and I had started doing it but the stepmother could see there was not any real punishment in it for us because we were so much bigger. She started making Joan do it instead. There were several times that I started to help Joan. Neither the oldest one nor the youngest one liked us helping. If we got caught or if someone squealed, the stepmother would whip Joan. If any of the suds were still visible, Joan had to redo the whole thing. Oh! How I hated times like these. The girls liked Joan doing their hair better then Karen or I because she was much gentler with them than Karen or I. I do not blame them for telling. I did blame them for causing Joan to get a whipping. I also blamed the stepmother for whipping Joan. Joan had to wash her own hair. The Stepmother's girls were both bigger then Joan and the same age.

Another thing our stepmother did, at the first of every month on a Saturday, she would go grocery shopping. Wow! It always looked like she bought out the entire store. It was more food than we had ever seen in our lives. The stepmother's food stamps bought the food. (Food stamps were another contention for a fight with her and dad.) We had never seen so much food all at once. In the beginning, it was great. We all pitched in and had it unloaded and put away in no time at all.

(One thing different between Grandma and the stepmother were, Grandma always said, "Do your work like you enjoy it. Find the easiest way of doing everything so that it is finished in half the time. This gives you more time to yourself.") Yes, it sounds selfish but that is what she taught us. Go with an attitude that you love everything and it will all go so much more smoothly. We tried to and it did seem to help.

The stepmother saw these things in us and she did not like us to enjoy ourselves. Yes in the beginning, we did not think of things as work. We thought everything was to have fun, to enjoy these things. We helped each other out by pitching in. This helped get it done quicker. Today they call this team work. The stepmother tried to reteach us that work was work; not for enjoying. Work was to be a punishment. For me I was too old to listen. It was hard for me to retrain myself.

I liked grandma's idea about work. To an outsider who did not understand why we acted as if we enjoyed everything. It would seem like we were always joking around and not respectful enough. We were just trying to make an impossible task seem better. It would also seem to an outsider that they were doing it deliberately to get out of work. Grandma would say, "There will be a lot of things that you will disagree with out there. If you can make the smaller task seem easier and make everything a game, life will be tolerable."

To the stepmother however it seemed that we thought life was one big game one big joke. We didn't we just wanted to enjoy life. She could not stand anyone who enjoyed himself or herself. She tried valiantly to reteach our way of thinking. She tried to turn our lives around. All I could do was stand by, watch, and listen.

Grandma's way of thinking I liked. The Stepmother however, seemed to get enjoyment out of watching us struggle. With me, I did not struggle too much. It did not faze me at all. I am not saying it was easy, but I managed it. I was able to put away these groceries without any trouble. I was five feet one and a half inches tall and pretty strong and surefooted. I was used to carrying babies on my hip. Fifty pounds of potatoes was not too much different. However my two younger sisters were tiny. As adults they never grew to five feet tall. As a child, they were very tiny and petite and still are today.

The stepmother would also buy cases and cases of number ten cans of different kinds of canned goods. I did struggle with these and I was older. They were heavy. I did manage it, but it was very difficult. She watched us every step of the way to make sure we did not drop it or carry in one or two cans at a time. We had a wagon and she would not even let us use it. She got tougher.

She started making Debbie do it. As an adult Debbie stands four feet nine inches tall, so as a ten-year-old child, she was very tiny. Debbie had spunk; she would do it just to spite the stepmother. Yes, she would.

Then it was Joan's turn. As an adult, she also stands four feet ten inches tall. As a small child of seven, she had a lot of trouble carrying in these fifty-pound bags of potatoes.

The cases upon cases were nearly impossible for her to carry. The step-mother saw how protective we were of each other. She watched Joan struggle every step of the way. If I had helped Joan, Joan would have gotten a whipping. We used to cry just watching these strug-gles and not being allowed to help. I did not understand how anyone could be so cruel. We did not mind helping each other. What is the big deal! We liked helping each other at least us younger ones did.

Oh God, how I cried and begged the stepmother to let me help carry in these groceries. I started hating grocery day. The stepmother stood guard over Joan every step of the way. She knew once her back was turned we would have helped Joan. We would have helped by carrying some of the heavier pieces for her. We would have lied saying, "No we did not help, Joan just walked faster than usual." On one occasion, we did assist Joan with carrying in the groceries. The stepmother saw us helping. Yes, Joan got a whipping. She still had to carry them in by herself. To this day, I do not understand how anyone can be so heartless. I do not understand how anyone can watch the struggles of a small child. It is beyond my comprehension.

As an adult when Joan was having babies (by this time she had already had two miscarriages. She was pregnant for a third time and was about to lose this one also.) She had a lot of trouble carrying a child full term.

She went to see a doctor, after the initial exam the doctor asked Joan what she did for a living. Joan said, "I am a secretary." The doctor said, "That would not cause the problems that I see." He said, "It would take a lot of heavy lifting." That is when Joan remembered her childhood. She told the doctor about all the heavy lifting of the groceries. The moving out of the refrigerator and stove, she was forced to do these chores every week, week after week as a young girl.

The doctor said, "That would certainly do it. When a female body was growing and going into puberty, it also is developing an area for the babies to lie." He also said, "Joan your body has a big hole where you should have developed the necessary equipment for carrying a child." He also informed her, the only way she would be able to carry a child would be to be bedridden the first six weeks to six months. He told her, "Do not carry anything or lift anything heavy the whole nine months." She had a beautiful baby girl. She has since then had a boy also. There were two more miscarriages since this time too. All because the stepmother for reasons we will never know made Joan do all this heavy lifting.

There were a lot of us. Why couldn't we help each other? We could get it done in half the time. It would have made it easier and it would have been fun, if you can call heavy lifting fun. This was probably the point it would have been fun.

It was one-hundred yards from the back of the car up steps to the kitchen. Then Joan carried the groceries through the door. She carried them down the basement. Canned goods were stored here.

I still do not understand what sadistic pleasure someone gets out of watching someone struggle, especially, when that person is a child.

# Food Poisoning

There was one time when the stepmother's mechanism backfired on her. Joan was required to do the dishes; Karen was still at home so Joan had to have been fewer than ten, being ten years younger than Karen is.

Joan washed all the dishes except one pan and she had left it on the stove. She had accidentally forgotten this pan. It was full of chicken and noodles. She not only forgot she did not know what to do with so much left over. It was a huge pan (we used to use a pan the size of an army kettle) much too large for a small child to have to tote and carry around. The Stepmother had left without giving instructions on what to do with the leftovers.

The next night for supper after sitting out all day and all night, we had to eat this chicken and noodles for supper. Without thinking, we started to eat. It not only smelled funny it tasted funny. At that time in our lives we had never heard of food poisoning but we have since this time. All of us took a bite, oh yuck! It tasted bad and it smelled. We said, "It tastes funny." The stepmother said, "Eat it anyway." The whole time while we ate supper she stood over us with a bullwhip. She did not leave the kitchen once. She wanted to make sure we ate every drop. She said, "Next time you won't be so careless as to leave food out all night, you will see to it that it is put away after every meal."

After all was quiet and everyone was in bed, suddenly one by one each one of us got sick. Fred was the first to get sick. He said, "I feel like I am puking my guts up." Karen and I were the last kids upstairs to get sick. Have you ever seen twelve kids trying to get over the same toilet at once? Oh! It was a sight all right and not very pretty. There was puke in the tub, puke in the sink. Some made it to the toilet. Some never made it anywhere except on the floor. If you have ever had food poisoning (the severe pain that suddenly strikes the pit of your stomach) it hurt so bad. Just thinking of it reminds me of the pain.

We made a lot of noise; so much so, that we woke dad up. Dad accused our stepmother of poisoning us or we would not all be sick at once. She did know too that we would be sick or she would not have stood over us to force us to eat this nasty smelling, foul tasting stuff. It was so curdled you could see bubbles on top and not from being too hot.

Your body will rid itself of the poison at all costs. All of a sudden, she remembered there were three younger children downstairs, just outside her bedroom. (I do not know why she had them sleeping downstairs she never heard them in the middle of the night.

Karen or I usually heard them wanting a bottle of milk or maybe just wanting to be rocked or cuddled.) This night, for the first time since moving in with us, our stepmother, had to take care of the three younger children all by her-self.

Karen and I were too sick to do anything. For the first time since she came along she had to do the dirty work, of cleaning the babies messes. She only did a superficial job to last until morning but do it she did. Most of us made it to the bathroom, but the younger ones were too little to get out of their cribs to go to the bathroom so they did it where they lay. They were one big mess from top to bottom. All fifteen of us kids got sick that night.

At the time, we did not know why but it did not take long to figure it out though. It is a wonder looking back not one of us was hurt. She was standing there with her whip in her hand forcing us to eat poisonous food. She knew exactly what she was doing. No one went to school the next day.

Joan however had to clean up the mess in the bathroom the next day and what a mess. This was her punishment for not putting the food away in the first place. Joan got sick all over again. Whew! The stench of that puke was so nauseating it was sickening. Dad again accused her of feeding us poison. He never once knew she had done so intentionally, no one had the guts to tell him.

If this had been the only time it had happened, it would have been differ-ent. There were other times when she tried and succeeded in getting us sick. There was also the time she had baked too many pumpkin pies for Thanksgiving dinner. A lot of them were still there one week later. We kept begging her to let us have a piece. She would not let us eat even one bite. It was not until they were starting to taste funny and there was mold growing on the tops of these pies, before she let us have a piece.

As an adult, I learned that pumpkin pies needed refrigeration, because of the milk contents in them. Well the stepmother baked so many pies there was not enough space in the refrigerator. She refused to waste anything except us kids. We had to eat these pies. Knowing there was mold growing on them. We had learned through health in school, that mold is a bacterial growth, not to be eaten and could make us sick. This time not all of us got sick, only a few of us, so dad could not blame her of poisoning us again.

We still have trouble eating pumpkin pie today because of this fiasco.

# Roaches

Each day brought on a new challenge. We had roaches all over the place. Everywhere you looked, there were many roaches. It was a creepy crawly feeling to have so many. You would turn on the light and it seemed like hundreds maybe even thousands would scatter everywhere.

One day, as soon as I had finished making chili for supper in our army size kettle there was a roach. One of those little critters was walking across the ceiling. It was moist up there on the ceiling from the steam of cooking. The roach lost its footing and plunk, it landed right smack dab in the chili. I was getting ready to take the roach out of the pot of chili. I was not going to tell anyone about what had happened. I was ready to eat the chili anyway even after picking out the roach.

The stepmother had ideas of her own. She walked in right then. She said, "Leave it in there! Do not take it out of there!" I was appalled. The thought of this roach getting into my bowl was most disgusting. It made me sick. Just the thought of leaving it there in the pot of chili turned my stomach. Not knowing where it was, was most intimidating to me.

As I dished out the bowls of chili for everyone, I put the roach in her bowl. My little sister Debbie was in the kitchen she thought it was a grand plan. The stepmother was about to take her first bite. She looked all around to see if anyone was going to scream out in alarm.

She almost did not see the roach in her bowl. When she did finally see it, there in her first bite she was mad, actually she was furious. She took her bowl of hot steaming chili and shoved it as hard as she could across the table. I sat directly across from her at the table. It landed in my lap. The chili was scalding hot. "Yowl!" It hurt pretty badly. I did not utter a sound. I blistered up on my belly, chest and legs but I did not care. I had the satisfaction of knowing I had made her mad. I had made her madder than she had ever been. She had made me mad. That is why I did what I did. I would have gladly eaten the chili without a fuss. I wanted to take the roach out before it was too late. I wanted it out before it added more germs to the chili but Noooo!! She had other ideas.

No one but Debbie knew of the plan ahead of time. When the other kids found out, they congratulated me. They said, "What an ingenious plan." I felt very good about pulling one over on her. The chili scalding me was well worth it.

There was another time I got the blame.

The stepmother found spinach on the table ledge underneath the table. Her kids' hated spinach but I loved spinach. I had to scrape the spinach off the table ledge. I had to eat this spinach. I do not know how many days the spinach had been sitting there. However, at this precise moment there were at least four roaches crawling all around on this slab of spinach. It was dried and crusty.

The stepmother said, "Norma Jean you get in here this instant." When she called your name like this you knew you were in trouble about something. She said, "You eat that spinach." I did not eat it at first after seeing the roaches crawling on it. I could not. I said to the stepmother, "I do not know why you are making me eat it. I love spinach. (Oh! Big mistake. I back talked. Smack! Smack!) It is your kids and some of my brothers and sisters that hate spinach." More back talk, smack! Smack! She got mad because not only was I disobeying a direct order but also I was blaming her kids.

She said, "You will eat it or I will shove it down your throat." Well I did not eat it. She did shove it down my throat. She grabbed the hair on the top of my head. She was pulling, and yanking as hard as she could. Then pried my mouth open with her fingers, and pushed the roach covered spinach into my mouth. I almost puked it back up in her face. I was gagging so badly. I was thinking about those roaches and trying figure out how long it had been sitting on that ledge. She smacked me as hard as she could again and held my mouth closed until I chewed and swallowed. I still love spinach. I cannot think of this scene when I eat spinach or I would not be able to eat spinach again.

I was furious. I never knew who did it. It was on the ledge by my seat at the table but I did not do it. The kids never told me who had done it. I think they all knew better. I told them (the stepmother's kids and my brothers and sisters heard me.)

If I ever had to eat stuff like that, again I would puke it up and make them eat it or shove it down their throats. Great threat too. I never saw another thing like that under the table.

Nevertheless, we also made a pact. If there was ever something for supper, that someone did not like. They should give it to someone who did like it. I said, "It is better the first time around than after roaches have crawled around on it."

I think me making that last statement as I did, helped to do wonders. We were passing food back and forth. I hated peas the stepmother's kids loved them. They hated spinach so I ate their spinach and they ate my peas.

It was a great system.

## Karen, Seen As A Threat

Right away, the new stepmother saw Karen as a threat to her authority. Everyone went to Karen with his or her problems. Her kids too started going to Karen with their problems. When they were hurt, they went to Karen. Some of her kids also started calling Karen mom. That was the last straw. She hated the very idea of her kids calling anyone but her mom. Therefore, she saw to it that Karen was not home most of the time, by either working at the department store, a local dry cleaning company, babysitting or doing odd jobs for the neighbors. She also saw that the house ran just as smooth with her as without her, so get rid of Karen and then the thread would weaken.

She had not counted that I was Karen's right hand.

I was an really good on handling situations as well but I was very young.

Karen was hardly ever home these days. She was always out of the house working and earning money. She was sixteen years old when our stepmother came along. We were used to running the house to grandma's specifications. How hard could it be to continue to run it in the same mode? We just had a lot more kids to keep things a little messier is all!

The stepmother was gone most of the time. We all had assigned chores to do. I had to make sure everyone did what he or she was supposed to do.

I was ten years old when I had this responsibility thrust upon me. To say that our house continued to run smoothly is a lie. It was a shambles. Oh! My brothers, sisters, and I got along great. The step-brothers, stepsisters, and I did not get along. They did not see me as an authority figure. Truly, I was a joke to them. I was not that much older than they were. I tried, do not get me wrong. However, there were six of us kids all the time. The older brothers and sisters of ours had to work. Junior and Vera had to leave the house they were too old to stay at home any longer, according to the stepmother. Karen worked. Larry and John had to help our dad at the garage. Then there were the five stepbrothers and stepsisters they seemed to see us all as a threat. We had a dad and they did not. They wanted our dad to be their dad. They forgot we did not have a mom. Actually, they did not care what we thought.

Until they moved in with us, they did not have a stable home life. It seemed they were moving every six to twelve months to get out of paying rent. The stepmother was on welfare and food stamps. She kept having children to get more money. By the time she got together with my dad, she had five children with four different men.

The stepmother purposely pitted us against each other.

Our stepmother's oldest son was mean. He hated all of us. Debbie, Freddie, and I were older than he was. Freddie was a joke to our stepmother. She could not even stand to look at him. Moreover, boys did not have to do housework. Housework was the girls' job in our house.

Our brothers helped us girls sometimes. The stepmother's sons did not help us at all. Her oldest was a boy. He was only six years old. He was used to watching all of his younger brothers and sisters when his mother was away. She was away a lot. He saw us as a threat to his authority over his brothers and sisters.

Oh, it took us a long time to come to some sort of peace. Actually, we never did come to a peace. It was quite a challenge. We were constantly fighting each other. We always had to do our chores and their chores in order to get things done in a timely manner. By five o'clock sharp chores had to be done. Supper cooked and on the table. The table set and ready to eat. The stepmother would walk in she expected things to be perfect. The dishes had to be washed and in the cupboard by six o'clock.

Then the challenge came.

The challenge was trying to get everyone to do his or her chores. I could not yell. I could not hit anyone. If I laid one finger on any of the kids, I got a beating. It was quite a challenge. Her children hated us.

If it were not for our brother Jimmy, her oldest son would have killed us. I could not tell you how many times Jimmy intervened on our behalf to keep us from the stepmother's oldest son taking a knife to all of us.

One day he threw me through a glass door. My bottom had a big gash on it. It still had glass in it. I had to have one of my younger sisters help me remove the glass and bandage it up. It should have had stitches. We were afraid we would all get a beating for letting this boy do what he did. Even though we had not control over him. Jimmy had to literally grab him and beat him up to make him leave me alone. Joan was bandaging me up. My scar is severe.

There was another time that he took a butcher knife to my sister Debbie. If Jimmy had not intervened, he would have killed Debbie with the butcher knife. He was that mean.

I still cannot believe that I was that afraid of this boy. He was the same age as Jimmy. They were both four years younger than I was. The stepbrother's dad was six feet four inches tall. This stepbrother was tall for his age. He was taller than any of us kids were.

The stepmother went through the house with a fine tooth comb. She put on white gloves and touched everything with her hand. Everything had to meet her specifications or we had to start all over again, if they were not. She inspected under the bed. Her kids had a way of just throwing things under the bed. We thought they did it on purpose just to get us into trouble. If one dish was dirty, she took every single dish, every single glass out of the cupboard and made us wash them again.

If it were not for my brothers, sisters, and I helping each other out we would never have survived this new set of tortures. I always thought that I took care of them but it was more like we took care of each other. We helped each other. We protected each other with this whole new set of rules and abuses that was being inflicted on us from this woman.

## Stepmother and Dad, Fighting

One day dad came home early. He had snuck up on us. We did not even hear his car pull in the driveway. When he walked into the house, we took off up the steps, out of sight out of mind. We wanted nothing to do with him. Naturally, he had been drinking. He started bellowing in the kitchen, "Woman! Where are you Woman?" None of us had any idea where she had gone. She had left earlier to go to the garage is what we supposed. She never told us where she was going, she just left. We had not seen her since. Of course, he would not have believed us even if we had told him. He was mad. He had been drinking heavier than usual.

By this time, we were all in the kitchen, by his order of course. Dad started slamming things around just being a terrifying bully. Finally, he saw the stepmother's oldest; he took him by the hair of his head and threw him into the back door, for nothing. He was somewhat staggering for a few seconds after he got up but get up, he did. God as my witness as much as I hated myself for it I was glad it was not me, dad had vented his anger on.

Finally, she comes in. She is mad as a hornet at what dad had done to one of her children and told him so. He said, "I do not care what you say about anything. I am going to have it out with you. I also want to know the name of your boy-friend." She said, "I do not have a boyfriend. Just because I am not putting out for you, you think I am putting out for someone else." In his current state, he did not believe anything. He proceeded to start beating and beating her; finally, he threw her across the kitchen. She landed in a heap; she was also seven and a half months pregnant with baby number six. She got up and stormed out of the house saying she was leaving. She said, "I am not going to take this shit anymore. I am going. I am never coming back." Before she left, she busted every window in dad's car. She wanted to give dad something to remember her by.

Dad was madder then I had ever seen him before. I remember him telling me he said, "Your stepmother is leaving me, this time for good. All because of this fictitious ghost everyone keeps seeing in you Norma." I did not say anything just stared at him. I hated him for blaming me for his problems. I hated everyone telling me how much I looked like my mother. I loved my mother. Then telling me it was my fault, no one could forget her. I was also hurt; all I ever wanted was for dad to love me in some small way. Instead of constantly telling how much trouble, just the sight of me caused some people. For our dad I guess it was too much to ask.

This time though I remember thinking that, at least with Grandma Lamb there was only one abuser because dad was hardly home. He left the responsibility of us kids to grandma. Now we had two abusers. Dad came home earlier than he ever had before.

I do not know why God wants us to endure all this. I keep praying it will stop.

At this time Larry said, "Ah! Come on dad give her time to cool off she will be back. Heck! She does not have any place else to go." Larry had been upstairs, thank heavens he had not heard everything dad had said. I was so horrified over the conversation with dad that I could not think straight.

Larry was right. The stepmother did eventually come back home. The damage she had done in the interim was immense. Dad was heartsick over the new endeavor of hers to get even. They continued to fight nonstop that summer. At least with them fighting each other they did not have much time to pick on us.

They hit us mostly when we happened to get in the way. Dad was so afraid she would leave him. We could not enjoy something. My younger brothers and sisters and I were not so lucky. She threatened a beating at every turn. Think it is a game, SMACK! Think it is funny, SMACK! All I could do is to stand and watch. We could do nothing. We all got the SMACK! SMACK! Think it is a game. No it was not a game. It was real life abuse and we were getting the brunt of their anger.

She got pregnant with number six because dad wanted her to. He told her she did not love him enough if she did not have his child. She could have all those other children without even being married.

They were usually fighting about something. The stepmother constantly accused my dad of having Ella (my mother) in their marriage. Saying she was a ghost. She was no longer around even if her kids were. She hated my resemblance to my mother. Apparently I looked so much like my mother that I could stop people, in their tracks, to stare at me. She thinks she hated it; well I had to live with it. Along with other peoples jealousy of it which usually turned to hatred. It also gave me an eerie feeling too, every time it happened to me.

I knew I was nothing like my mother; she was good, pure, loving, and kind. I had evil thoughts all the time. I started resenting the stepmother for everything. I became obstinate. Oh! I still did the household chores like cooking, cleaning, and taking care of the kids. I hated her for hating my mother. Who was no longer around to defend herself!

I did not understand about haunting memories, not really.

There were some times however, on special occasions dad took us to the cemetery. He helped us give flowers to our mother. I never knew if it was because he still loved her or if it was for us kids. It was a special time only him and us kids understood. The stepmother went the first time; after that, she refused to go. Dad went anyway. He took us kids once more. They had a big fight about it and the stepmother told dad to go by himself.

She said, "She was his children's mother now and they had better start treating her as such." She never once gave us any respect. Just hollering, bellowing, and barking orders to get this job done or that job done.

Not too much time passed that one of the stepmother's son, was trying to get her attention. He said, "Mom, mom, mommy, MOMMY," (he was pulling and tugging on her skirts the whole time which should have drawn her attention also) but did not, finally he screamed, her first name. That got her immediately attention, she smacked him right across the face, with all the force she could muster. He was around three; he went flying across the kitchen floor. She said,

"If you ever call me that again I'm going to whip you. I am your mother and that's what you will call me." She never once apologized. It was her fault to begin with because she would not pay any attention to him. Just smacked him, and he went flying across the room with a bloody lip.

Within the week, we were sitting around the kitchen table, all sixteen of us; fourteen kids and two adults. (the baby had not been born yet) Dad told us, he said, "From here on out you will call your stepmother mom or mother." Boy, the resentments started, with that announcement, no one said anything. Furthermore dad said, "you will call her mom or else." We all knew what the or else was we did not need to be told, the or else would have been a whipping. No one called her by her given name ever again. Neither did we call her mom. We could not. Not once did she so much as ask us to do so. She just demanded it of us so that her own kids would not call her by her given. No! She could not do that. She did not feel she needed our respect. She just demanded it of us. We could not. It seemed like the harder we tried to call her mom, the more we seemed to choke on that very word.

We very seldom tried to get her attention drawn to us. We made sure we were close enough for her to hear and just begin a conversation. Once I made the mistake of saying, "hey you." Never in my wildest dreams did I ever think the repercussions would have been so severe. She smacked me as hard as she could land the palm of her hand. It was a powerful hand it hit and numbed the whole side of my face. I could not call her by her given name. I choked on the word mother. I felt my mother was dead. My mother was loving and kind everything that this woman was not. I just could not force myself to call her mom.

# The Laundromat

Before we got a stepmother, we had a washer and a dryer. When she came along, she bought a brand new set. The old one was not good enough for her clothes. Then she would not let us use the washer and dryer again. She said, "None of your filthy, dirty, stinky clothes are going into my new machines." She had never owned a washer and dryer before she moved in with us, now she made us go to the Laundromat.

At first, she made us go to the Laundromat once a month. Can you imagine clothes lying on the damp cement basement floor, for a month how they would smell, especially when two to three of the kids wet the beds. Plus we had fifteen kids in our house to take to the Laundromat.

She also expected us to wear our clothes for a week before changing. The kids at school laughed at us, but worst of all it was very unsanitary. When a teenager is starting to change, they start to sweat a lot more than usual too. She made all of us wear our clothes more than once I never did it again. The stepmother did not care about anything except the amount of money we spent washing clothes. As if she was earning the money, she moved in, took over, and started spending dad's money and we had to start using the Laundromat.

Neither Karen nor I would wear our clothes for a week. We refused; we stuck to our guns. Neither did we keep our clothes in the basement to rot or to stink. We did one more thing too we washed our clothes separate. We just could not help it. We had to buy all our own clothes. Our (outside) babysitting money paid for them. Therefore, we took care of ours separately. We had to do the washing. It was a nightmare, going to the Laundromat, we would hand carry the clothes over in baskets.

In the summer, we had to carry them back home, wet so that we could hang them on the clothesline and they were heavy. There were so many baskets, at least ten, or fifteen and we carried each one of them. After a while, we got smart and pulled the wagon, but not all would fit, so we still had to carry a few baskets as well.

The nightmare however was that every time we went to the Laundromat the clothes reeked of the basement after a month of laying on the floor, yuck! There were also maggots, silverfish, and roaches crawling around. People would go running when they saw us coming up the street, they recognized us. After months of doing it this way the attendant told our stepmother she was going to have to do the laundry more frequently. (How embarrassing and our class mates laughed when they saw us too.) He said, "He could not have us running off his other customers." He also said, "If you cannot do it more frequently then find yourself another Laundromat." Well that settled it because she wasn't about to find another Laundromat since this one was so convenient, she never once in all the years of us doing laundry there did she ever offer to take us in a car. We had to sort, stack, fold, iron, dry, and everything else imaginable there is for the clothes not once did she offer assistance. She also expected us to keep hers and dad's laundry done up, oh yeah, for their clothes we could use the washer and dryer in the basement.

In the beginning, we hated washday until we got smart. Then we had a ball. This was after Karen was no longer helping. We would load up the washers and then run off to play for about twenty to thirty minutes. By the time we came back, the washers were done and ready for the dryer. Then we would load up the dryers doing the same and put in a few extra coins for good measure. Except on those days, we had to carry them home to put them on the clothesline.

When the stepmother found out we were having fun at her expense she got really mad. She found a branch off of a tree and hit each one of us all the way back to the Laundromat. You see she was mad because we were supposed to be working, doing the laundry, but the laundry was doing itself. She was home babysitting. She did not like it one bit. It was well worth it in the end. We had few precious moments where we were just kids, without a pack of kids to oversee.

One thing we did learn though was post a guard. The guard watched the road. We took turns being guard. We wanted to make sure one person was not always stuck being the guard. We had signals to signal the others. It was different every time. Someone ran and told the other. As she came in on direction we came in the other with our new system.

Most of the time I volunteered to be guard because I felt I was too big for the swings on the playground. I was thirteen. I also volunteered to continue putting clothes into the dryer and keeping an eye on things, so all the others could play longer.

You see John Burroughs Elementary was real close by and they had a playground for kids to enjoy. So we were not out causing trouble we were truly having some kid fun.

## Being Forced to Play Outside

There were many radical changes when the stepmother came into our lives. We had a baby in diapers, a mother whom resented us and whom we must have resented. Two stepbrothers, three stepsisters and she was about to give us another baby for us to take care of. With so many children from two different families in the house there was always a fight going on. Someone was always mad at someone.

It seemed the harder we tried to clean the house; keep it clean to please the stepmother, it was never good enough. The second winter, with the stepmother acting the part of our mother was probably one of the most agonizing winters we ever lived through. Our half-brother was born this winter, so the stepmother was home a lot. She was too pregnant to go anywhere. Our dad was mean when he was drinking. When he was not drinking we loved him. He was a very nice man and a good father. It was just that he could not stay sober for long. The step-mother however was mean through and through. There was not a nice bone in her body. She would just as soon beat us as to look at us.

Even when I would try to think of a logical reason for the things, the step-mother did to us kids while we were living with her. I cannot come up with even one that makes any sense. This winter she threw us outside day in and day out all day long. Now in the summer-time when the weather was nice and warm she would not let us go outside to play. I remember some of the kids beg-ging and begging to go outside and play. Going outside to play is a normal kid thing to do. All kids want to play outside when it is warm. This past summer and she would not let us.

Now that it is sub-zero outside, we have to go outside and play. We would go out around nine o'clock in the morning and could not come back inside until six o'clock that evening.

I remember the time so well, because our oldest sister Karen would leave for work. That would be when the stepmother made us go outside, and when she came home, we went back inside. I don't think she wanted Karen to know because she knew Karen would tell our dad.

If we had to go to the bathroom, we had to wet our pants. We could not get a drink of water; we could not go to the bathroom; we could not get anything to eat. We just plain and simple could not go back inside the house. Now we were begging and begging to go back in the house.

This was our punishment for wanting to play outside in the summertime. The stepmother would laugh and say, "What are you crying about all summer long you begged to go out and play. Now I am letting you outside to play. All you want to do is huddle out there, as if you are cold. Now you are crying, I wanna come in." Three kids did not have to go out. They were the three youngest ones including the newborn baby. Oh! How I hated her at times like these. I would wish it was her doing these things she was making us do. Sub-zero weather no hats, no gloves hardly a coat worth calling a coat. Wet pants after eight hours of standing in the cold, even the heartiest soul will eventually wet themselves and that in itself is humiliating.

Finally one day some police officers happened to be driving by and heard all the crying and wailing we were doing. They went to investigate the situation. The police officers told the stepmother to let us go inside out of the cold. As soon as the police officers left, though she made us go back outside. I think even her own kids despised her then, because they were forced to endure the same treatment as we were enduring. The neighbors called the police a second time. The same thing happened.

The second summer with the stepmother, she boarded up all the windows upstairs and nailed them shut. We could not even get any fresh air. Then she painted them shut. The glass too was painted. We could not even see any sunshine or see the flowers bloom or anything. It served two purposes it saved on money so that she would not have to buy curtains. She wanted none of the neighbors to see inside our house. She did not want to have to spend money on frivolous things like curtains, sheet, bedspreads, and clothes for us kids. Even though it was dad's money, she was spending. She wanted it all spent on herself. She never bought us clothes only the things given to us by neighbors and friends.

Then the kids at school would laugh and poke fun and say "Hey that's my old dress. What are you doing with it?" How embarrassing!

# Red Hot Temper

One Sunday afternoon Karen and I cooked dinner. Normally this would have consisted of twenty pounds of potatoes, eight chickens, and six big #10 cans of corn. Karen and I cut up and flowered the chickens, peeled and mashed the potatoes there was not any help from anyone else, (not yet anyway, as we aged others took over or helped out) after all this, we were allowed to sit down and eat.

The stepmother liked to eat.

Nothing and no one kept her from eating. At this time the youngest, her sixth child was old enough to eat table food but not feed himself so this made two kids in high chairs. Well this particular Sunday, she got mad because she could not take a bite, without giving two bites away. Both kids in the high chairs were hungry. She got so mad she literally flung both high chairs backwards at once. She did not have full control of her own children even, half the time. She could not even feed them once without getting mad. She said, "I am the mother and all of you sit there and eat, while I have to feed these babies. No more will I feed them. Karen you stop eating and feed them." Neither Karen nor I waited for her to finish her speech, to get up and comfort the babies; it was an automatic reflex action on our part. We got up comforted, cleaned, and fed them. She never once stopped shoveling food into her own mouth to make sure the kids were okay.

Yes! I can honestly say I had no love for this woman who would treat her own children, with such disregard. From that day forward, her youngest daughter was old enough to feed herself, she sat at the stepmother's end of the table. The youngest boy sat on the same end as Karen, while Karen fed him, before she could eat herself. It turned out great on the stepmothers end; she was able to continue to stuff her face first, foremost and always.

The best food was always on her plate. She and dad ate eggs, bacon, toast, or sausage for breakfast. We ate whole grain long cooking oats, very nasty tasting stuff, very lumpy too, if not cooked just right. It was the commodities brand of oats we ate, not the store bought quick oats. We seldom had sugar for our cereal. We were only allowed to use powdered milk, and never got to use whole milk.

Our lunches consisted either of cheap bologna or cheap braunsweiger, plain or with butter. After eating either of these sandwiches, you always had to burp. Loud obnoxious burps! The burps were so nasty it stunk up the whole classroom. Naturally the kids all knew who had burped, looked at me and started laughing. There was never any mustard, mayonnaise, or ketchup. If one sandwich was not enough to fill you up, we were allowed two and nothing else.

Personally, I could not stomach either breakfast or lunch so I usually went without. Oh! Believe me the stepmother made sure we left home with our lunch. A beating was waiting if we tried to leave it behind. That did not mean I could not throw it away once out of sight or at school. There is always a trash can out there somewhere, so I usually went hungry. I just was not used to this kind of treatment or this kind of food. It was very unappetizing to me.

Then there were the potatoes. After peeling twenty pounds of potatoes, at least three times a week a person did not care how thick the skin was. Well the stepmother cared. After we peeled the potatoes, she went through the skins. Every single time we peeled potatoes she went through the skins, to make sure that the skin and only the skin was removed, and not one part of the potato. Many times, we had to peel the skin away from the peeling because it was too thick, according to what she thought it should be.

She smacked us when we left any of the runny white in the shell of an egg. She would dig it out of the trash and make us use it. Once I made that fatal error in judgment. Once smacked you never do it again. My nose was numb. I had to dig it out of the trash and had to watch dirty, trashy, stuff go into the food I was making, I almost vomited on the spot and all she did was laugh.

You finally learn self-preservation first, foremost and always.

I told you earlier that dad ran his shop seven days a week. Well when the stepmother came along she insisted he close up on Sundays. He did. Sundays were sometimes fun or became so. We watched movies; John Wayne movies, Shirley Temple movies, Hercules, or whatever movies happened to be on at the time. It was somewhat fun. There usually was not any yelling on Sundays. Dad stayed sober.

The stepmother usually took a nap. It was very enjoyable. Now if by chance someone accidentally woke her up it became very tense. She would start shrieking at the top of her lungs. She shrieked at anyone and everyone. Then we had to go upstairs to bed in the middle of the afternoon, no matter what the season. No matter what time it was. Oh! How I hated it. Especially in the summertime when the sun was still shining, we would have to go to bed, so much for an enjoyable Sunday afternoon.

It was without supper too. We got out of cooking, but we did not get supper either.

One day when we went to the pool, the stepmother said, "Do not go swimming right away. Wait until the younger kids are ready." Well Larry could not wait. The stepmother went down to the side of the pool and pulled Larry out by his hair, in front of everyone. She said, "I said, no one was to go swimming until all the younger ones were ready to go. No! You, Larry go deliberately against my wishes. You just couldn't wait." During this whole tirade, she was yelling at the top of her lungs in front of every-one. She was not only embarrassing all of us, making a fool of herself. She did not stop there the tirade continued, she said, "Furthermore since you deliberately disobey my orders, you can sit out for a while. You just cannot follow orders can you." The degradation, humiliation, and mortification Larry felt was tremendous. He laughed or rather shrugged it off but you know it had to have hurt very deeply. Heck, here he was going to school five days a week, on the honor roll, working at the garage to help dad make ends meet. He did all this without pay. He was on the wrestling team. He was on the track team. He did pretty well on both of these too. He was an all-around American boy in spite of his circumstances.

He finally gets a few minutes to himself and she has to spoil it for him. I just do not understand why a parent, even a step-parent would do these kinds of things, or why ours did these things to us. Larry did not mean any harm. He really loved to go swimming; she did not have to go off the deep end.

It was a very seldom rare treat to be able to do anything fun.

## No Boyfriends Allowed

I was fourteen years old when, I got the beating of my life. I let a boy-friend into the house while my stepmother and my dad were not at home. This I knew was a very big no-no! He was helping me to baby-sit. I was the oldest of twelve now and a girl. I was always watching my younger brothers and sisters and there were five of them. My step-mother had her five kids that I watched. In addition, I watched my half-brother. There were twelve kids myself included. My stepmother gave me the responsibility of baby-sitting all my younger brothers and sisters plus her six children. Some-times they would not listen to me. Debbie especially, because she was only eighteen months younger, "why didn't she get to baby-sit instead of me," was what she was always whining?

"Norma J-e-a-n!" When our step-mother screamed your first name, you knew you were in trouble. When she yelled your second name and accentuated each syllable of your name. Your ass was grass. Then when she yelled your second name with a high pitched squealing stretched like a balloon you knew you were in dire straits. You should have gotten there yesterday.

"What in the hell is the meaning of this." As she takes Debbie's hair and parts, it away from her forehead to show me where Debbie's hair was missing a good one-inch section of her hair. I thought, how did she find out? It was right in front. I thought we had done a good job of hiding it. Someone must have told. Who would have told?

"How did this happen?" She asked.

I said, "I don't know." Smack! I knew I was a goner if I told her what really happened.

She asked again, "How did this happen?"

I said, "I don't know." Smack! Smack! This time I got two smacks on the face. It stung. My ears were already ringing. There was a deep red mark on my face. It stung that bad. You could even see the imprint of her fingers on my face that is how hard she slapped me.

Again she asked me, "How did this happen?" During this whole scenario, Debbie is watching and not saying a word. Finally, I caved in and told her. I said, "George pulled Debbie's hair out."

She hollers, "Who in the hell is George?"

I said, "My boyfriend."

The stepmother said, "What in the Sam Hell were you doing with a boy-friend in the house while we were gone? What were you two doing?" Smack! Smack! Smack! Up to three smacks now.

I said, "Nothing, he was helping me to baby-sit."

She said, "Like hell he was."

I thought how was I, going to sneak off and do something; even some-thing as small as kissing, when there were eleven sets of prying eyes watching me every second. There was no way to sneak off, with that many kids around there is no such thing as privacy. Nevertheless, he was helping me to baby-sit. My younger brothers and sisters did not see me as an authority. Some of my younger brothers and sisters thought I was a joke. The ones younger than me thought I was a joke, not all of them. Some were model citizens for me and this helped a lot. I could count on them to help. The stepmother's kids did not see me as an authority either. I was a joke to them. I was the oldest of these twelve. The youngest was our one-year-old half-brother. No way was there any privacy for hanky-panky.

"Why was George here? Don't tell me it was to help you baby-sit, because I do not believe it, for one second."

"It's the truth!" I was crying by this time. I could see out of the corner of my eye Debbie was starting to chuckle a little. She had that little smirk on her face when she had just gotten out of trouble herself. (Nerves can do this make you chuckle or smile at inappropriate times. But I did not know this back then.) It never dawned on me who had told. I had always blamed the stepmother's kids. It made me feel ashamed and guilty.

That chunk of Debbie's hair was still missing. I did not blame her for liking the fact of me getting into trouble. It was as much as I deserved. I knew it would never happen again having a boyfriend in the house. No one would get the chance to rip out someone else's hair. I truly felt awful and hated myself for allowing it to happen.

"Debbie you go on upstairs. Norma you go and sit on the bench." I did go and sit on the bench too and Debbie went upstairs to the bedrooms. The stepmother came into the kitchen and she said, "When your father gets home you are going to get a beating from your Father and me." To say I was scared was putting it mildly. I was scared to death about the whole thing. Getting an instantaneous beating is one thing but to think about it for a few hours was almost unbearable.

As the dreaded hour approached, I was, dreading it more and more. I knew Larry and John had both gotten beatings before. So I went to both of them and asked them how did they do it? How do you make it through the beating without it hurting and without crying? They both said they put a book inside their pants so they would not feel anything. They said whatever you do; do not cry that will make it a whole lot worse. They love to see you cry.

Well I knew a book would not help me. Girls did not wear jeans or pants back then. We could only wear dresses. Under-pants would not hold a book. I started praying and praying that God would not allow me to cry. I prayed He would not allow me to feel anything at all so that I could face the beating. I knew I did deserve some kind of punishment for the treatment of my little sister. I truly was sorry. I was crying silently living through the devastation of what had happened to Debbie all over again and it was my fault.

With this many children in the house we had a good-sized dining room table and it was sturdy. A big person could lay on it without doing any damage to it. I was five foot one and a half inches tall and I weighed ninety-five pounds. My stepmother was five feet five and a half inches tall and weighed around one hundred and fifty pounds. My dad was five feet ten and a half inches and weighed two hundred and fifty pounds. When they took the notion to beat you, you knew you were getting a beating.

I had a few hours to think about my punishment. The big hour was finally here. I kept hoping they might forget. The stepmother made sure Dad had gotten home early from the garage.

After supper the stepmother said, "Norma lie on the table and grab the table with both hands." I did. My legs were dangling. My arms were wide to both sides of the table. I started praying again to God to help keep me from crying. I am waiting for the beating.

One, two three, I was going to count them to keep myself from crying. This would give me something to do. I know this came from God! I knew God was with me, He sent me Jesus. Jesus was going to keep me company, during this whole ordeal. Thank you, Jesus! Four, five, six, it was hurting bad already. This was just the beginning. We got beatings with a rubber hose from a car. The step-mother and dad had taken this one inch in diameter hose, small enough to make it flexible. They sliced through it all the way down to a handle the size for a hand. Then they took these two half's and cut them in half again to make four long pieces of rubber with which to whip you with. Seven, eight, nine, the whole time I was getting a beaten I was counting, I needed something to distract me. Ten, "dammit" the stepmother had just hit herself with the hose. Eleven, twelve, thirteen, fourteen, these were extra hard because she had hit herself with the hose. It must have hurt her, and she was mad. As these pieces of rubber hit any part of your body, it stung. As it went away from your body, it ripped a piece of skin with it. It was starting to bleed. It was starting to leave big welts on my back, arms and legs they were starting to go numb. The rubber hose seemed to split the clothes on my back. Those places it did not rip started sticking to my back. I could feel the blood oozing it was starting to trickle down my legs where it had ripped open. My arms were hurting from the beating and from hugging the table to keep from crying. I did not cry. I know God was helping me, to keep me from crying. Twenty, twenty-one, twenty-two, twenty-three, I started thinking when the step-mother was up to twenty-two that it was also times four, that would make it eighty-eight, no wonder it hurt so bad. Thirty, thirty-one, thirty-two, I was not crying yet. I was still praying . Forty-eight, forty-nine, fifty when will she quit. "There that's done!"

"Arthur! You get your ass in here right this minute." Another one of those high-pitched squeals she used them on him too. It is your turn. I could tell she was elated. She was enjoying herself ordering us all around like puppets. I did not know if I could take another fifty lashings without crying. The fifty I already had times four was already up to two hundred. My body already felt raw and tingly. Now dad was going to put his arm into some more beatings. I had to do some more praying and quick if I wanted to make it through this set too. I saw dad's face just before he took over. All the things he had done to us were never this bad. It was as if he was apologizing and agonizing over it all with just that one look. The look that said he was sorry before he got started. He did it anyway. The stepmother had done this to him. He could not stand up to her anymore. One, two, three, here we go again. God you have to send me Jesus again, I need Him to be here again, quick. Thank you for not letting me cry. Jesus, thank you for helping me again I need you here. I know that without you I could not go through all this. Ten, eleven, twelve, I wonder when he would quit the stepmother was standing over him the whole time to make sure he did not quit, beating me. He was never home this early on a weeknight she must have made him come home early. Forty-eight, forty-nine, fifty the stepmother said, "Ok Arthur that is enough. I think she gets the message she will not have boyfriends in the house now. Will you Norma?"

I said, "No!" Now that it was over, I could barely walk. I wanted out of their sight. I was shaking uncontrollably. I felt ashamed that I could not control the tears now that it was over. I was not crying exactly, tears were there, there just was not any sound. I got to thinking about how many times my dad had hit me. It was another fifty times. Four times that made it two hundred plus the two hundred from the stepmother that made four hundred. No wonder I am shaking so bad.

I did not get to lay around the house either and feel sorry for myself. I had my regular household chores to do. I did them. I made sure the kids were ready for bed. The rest of the day, I stayed in my room. I knew all eyes would be on me. Some would think I deserved it, and then others would have pity.

I did not think I could handle the looks of sympathy I would get. I would have cried than for sure.

The next day came and I went back to school as usual. I had trouble sitting down in the seats. The bleeding had stopped and the scabs made it hard to sit without it pulling on my skin. It would just start bleeding all over again.

Today they sent reminders home tomorrow was picture day. The stepmother loved this part, all of her children and stepchildren getting pictures for the Grandparents.

I took my letter into the house. That night she cut my hair. She said, "The beating was for having the boyfriend in the house, now the hair cut was for letting your boyfriend pull that inch of Debbie's hair out."

The beating was for my soul. Jesus helped me. The haircut was out there for all to see. You could not hide this.

I looked into the mirror and did not know how I was going to straighten out this mess. I did not pray to God this time though. Grandma taught us vanity was a sin. I looked ugly. My haircut was a mess. I felt I did deserve it though. I did cry this time. If the beating was not enough well this certainly did the trick. Karen came into the bathroom and between the two of us managed to make some order out of the butchered haircut. Karen cried with me. It was that horrible.

Thank you again Karen for making a little bit of a difference to a messy haircut. I may not have told you then but I am telling you now.

Thank you God! Thank you Jesus, for being there in my hour of need!

# A Child's Nervous Breakdown

The stepmother had a way of badgering you and badgering you until you finally would break down. She would badger you until you told her a few of the facts, not the real facts just something to get her off your back. This is how she would get someone to tell on others or themselves. This is how the truth came out on the eventful day of my beating. It was because of her my sister said what my boyfriend had done and I got the beating.

It was just another sign of how the stepmother pitted one of us against the other. Whether it was with our brothers and sisters or the stepbrothers and stepsisters, who were involved, she pitted each one of us against the others. She manipulated everything in the house to her specifications.

At that time, the pain was still too fresh in my memory. It was not a thing to get over that easily. What I did not know was, during this episode in our life one of my siblings would have a nervous breakdown. At the age of twelve, they did not deal well at all with this kind of pressure or stress.

I did not know who had told on me until years later, after we became adults.

I relived the nightmares repeatedly. (I would sit down in a school chair, my dress would ride up and the kids would ask, "what happened to you" or "where did you get that ugly bruise" or what happened to your hair.") I was so humiliated and embarrassed all over again. I would wear long sleeves shirts and long socks to hide all the marks.

After a while, when I heard they had a nervous breakdown my little bit of trouble did not seem to be so severe. Not as bad as having a nervous breakdown, I was able to forgive and forget. Looking back the depression I was in was also a nervous breakdown just not as severe. I at least was functional if not emotionally at least physically functional.

It was just hard for me to have close friends because of the entire trauma and still is today. I do not know whom to trust.

My sibling ended up in the hospital. It was not until adulthood and into counseling that they even knew, they had a nervous breakdown. The doctor sent for medical records as an adult. The doctor found out the diagnosis from that long ago hospital stay. I was able to forgive and forget because I realized the traumas they too had suffered because they too had been just a child.

The deep dark secret happened to be the most obviously traumatic. They were afraid of entering puberty. At this time, they were even afraid of their own shadow. All the things we had suffered up to this point and the things we saw our own brothers and sisters suffer were just too much for us to deal with anymore.

By the time they were twelve going on thirteen, they had epileptic like seizures. It was not epilepsy but the seizures were very similar. They would start all of a sudden, for no apparent reason their body would just start shaking uncontrollably; then fall to the floor; the body instinctively would curl up into a fetal position. Finally after about four or five of these seizures, they went to the hospital, to get tests ran. The doctors ran every test in the book and could find no apparent reason for these seizures.

The doctors could not find anything wrong until, while still in the hospital, an old man tried to molest them, right in their hospital bed. They fought the old man off as best they could but the molester was very strong.

The stepmother, dad, and Grandma Baas walked in just as he was attacking them. The old man took off. The grown-ups started laughing instead of trying to protect this child. The stepmother said, "Ha! Ha! So now, we know why you wanted to come to the hospital. You wanted to be raped." This brought an even greater roar from the three-some. It was just too much to deal with. This child not only did not feel safe at home in her own bed, now had to face things like this in the hospital. The adults that were supposed to protect, laughed instead of helping. This sibling started having seizures in the hospital (stress-related?) Today it would be called post-traumatic stress disorder.

I cannot understand the stepmother feeling this way, even though we were only her stepchildren. But for a grand-mother and a dad to laugh and think it is funny is beyond my comprehension. They did not even try to go after that man and press charges.

When this child did finally come home from the hospital the stepmother said, The seizures are caused by them needing attention. (The stepmother didn't even have the decency to call them sei-zures. She called them attention fits.) So whenever a seizure happens to attack, give them the attention they deserve. She said, "Just laugh! This will make the fits go away. It will help because attention is all they need."

We believed the stepmother too. These seizures were pretty scary. We wanted to help.

We gave them attention, just the worst kind. The kind that the stepmother said she needed. It was the worst kind that one could possibly ask for at a time like this. We did laugh, poke fun of, and humiliate them. This was what we were told was needed. While we were poking fun at this one, it kept the others from poking fun at us. We did not realize that this kind of attention was not what was needed. The stepmother knew these things. She saw the medical report and talked to the doctor. The doctor talked to them to show them the seriousness of the situation.

As an adult and through counseling the real reason came out about the breakdown. The doctor sent for the medical records from the time spent in the hospital, the results were profound. The doctor found a twelve year old having a nervous breakdown, caused by the environment in which they lived.

The doctors had told  both the stepmother and Dad the results.

For the wellbeing of this child, it is imperative they leave this environment and go somewhere else, to a different environment from which she lives.

The stepmother and Dad did not listen to a thing the doctor had to say. They thought it was preposterous.

My sibling has come a long way since this time. At least now, we know the reasons behind the fears and anxieties.

# Dad's Illness

It has been five years since our dad married our stepmother. It has been a struggle too for all of us. We had trouble surviving what we have been through up until now.

It was the summer before Larry's senior year of High School. Dad was complaining about back pain. Dad never complained about pain. Since dad was complaining, you knew he was in a lot of pain.

They only had two VA Hospitals at this time in Ohio, one in Cleveland, and one in Cincinnati. Both of these two hospitals were two and a half hours away, it made these two hospitals too far away. They were in the process of building one in Dayton, which was going to be a whole lot closer. The stepmother wanted dad to wait until February to go to the doctor's office. She wanted him to wait until the Dayton office was open. That is exactly what they did. It would be open in February of the following year.

It took six or seven months for dad to go to the hospital. If dad had gone when he first started complaining about being in a lot of back pain the results may have been different. My dad usually did not want to go to the Doctor's office or the hospital. He rarely complained about being in pain.

When dad finally did get to go to the hospital they had him in within the week for surgery. They said, "This man is in terrible shape."

Dad had a massive amount of tumors in the small of his back. The doctors removed the tumors. His stomach had cancer. They removed forty percent of his stomach. The colon had cancer; they removed sixty percent of his colon. The doctors moved his esophagus from the center of his body to his side. Dad was in a lot of pain. He was no longer drinking anything at this point. He was in the hospital a very long time.

When dad finally came home from the hospital, he was not home long, before he went back into the hospital.

(The day he came home from the hospital he gave one of his sons a beating. I will explain more later in the next chapter.)

He was in about a week this time.

When he came home, us girls, Debbie, Joan, and I had to cook special meals for dad. He was on a special diet. He kept complaining that we were not cooking it properly. He said, "What are you trying to do, kill me." We were trying really hard to do it right.

The stepmother did not leave us any instructions on how to cook dad's meals. The doctors told her at the hospital how to go about preparing these special meals but she never told us. It was trial and error for us. Then dad started complaining that his food did not have any taste. He blamed us for this also. We did the best we could. There were no instructions given on what kinds of spices to use. We were told no salt from dad himself. More than once, he threw the food at us. We had a mess to clean up as well. Food splattered everywhere. He hit us for not getting it right.

Dad was wasting away. He went from two hundred and fifty pounds to one hundred and twenty five pounds in a matter of weeks. To us girls he really looked sick. We whispered to each other what we thought. Even Jimmy was involved in this conversation. We did not know what was going to happen to us if something happened to our dad.

The stepmother was gone a lot. She was now supervising the garage. Larry had been running the garage since he was little with very little supervision from dad. Larry knew how to run the garage. He did not need supervising. The stepmother just wanted to make sure she got the money. She did not want Larry to reinvest it into more parts.

Dad could not get comfortable either. His back was starting to hurt him from lying around. He was in a lot of pain too from all the surgery's he'd had. We started rubbing his back to make him feel better. We would fluff up his pillows still he complained.

Dad was in so much pain that he once asked us to take a hammer to him and kill him. We were devastated. We were afraid he was dying.

He did finally tell us once, he was sorry for complaining so much. He said,

"I know you guys are trying real hard to get it right. I appreciate it." He also told us we were doing better than the nurses were." He said, "He was thankful for children like us who were trying to please him."

I thank God for allowing me to hear these words even if at the time I was not ready to hear them. God kept them in my heart. He knew I would need them later. He knew I would remember them when I was ready to hear them.

## John gets a Beating

The day dad got home from the hospital the stepmother told dad everything that had been going on, since he had been in the hospital. For one thing, my brother John had always been an unruly child. As a teenager, he was atrocious and why not, he had prime examples in his so-called parents.

John was out of school more than he was in school from being suspended and from skipping school. He was smoking and drinking on the school grounds. He was caught shoplifting and had been put in jail, until Grandma Lamb bailed him out.

The icing on the cake was he was caught seducing the neighborhood girls. The girls' parents had to inform the stepmother of his deeds. They wanted retribution. One of the things they wanted was John sent to boy's industrial school. The stepmother assured the girls parents she would have John taken care of (a beating).

The stepmother also found out John had been having sex with two of her own girls. Somehow, her girls were hood winked into telling on themselves.

She told the neighbors and her daughters that she would see to it that John was whipped. She would have whipped John herself but she knew if she tried John would have taken the whip away from her. He would have used it on her instead. He would get that mad. For some reason John had an undying respect for our dad. It could have been simply because he was our dad.

The very day dad came home from the hospital the stepmother insisted dad whip John. Even after all that extensive surgery, he had just undergone. He still had not recuperated.

Dad did not want to but the stepmother insisted. Even though, he did not quite feel up to it. She said, "If you do not whip him I'm going to have him put away someplace like the Boys Industrial School." Well that did the trick. Dad had not been through all the things he had been through just to lose his kids now. He did as the stepmother demanded.

He did a damn fine job too; he must have been hoping to beat some sense into John. It was one of the worst beatings, any of us kids ever got.

John was bleeding over every square inch of his skin that was exposed, his face was bleeding, and his mouth was bleeding. His nose and ears were bleeding. I helped to clean him up but he looked awful. John had gotten beat so bad he could not walk. He had to crawl on his hands and knees to get into bed.

He was crying. Dad had beaten him within an inch of his life. It was horrible, John kept saying to dad, "I'm sorry Daddy, I'm sorry. I'll never do it again, I promise."

For John to cry was a miracle. For him to beg and promise not to do it again was another miracle. John had meant every word he had said too; unfortunately the next day dad was back in the hospital. The exertion dad had done while beating John had caused some new trouble, dad was hemorrhaging. He was in a week this time.

John blamed himself for dad having to go back into the hospital. When dad came home this time, he did not do anything at all just laid around in bed.

John was depressed and despondent. He felt like a real heel. He did his best to make up to dad for causing him to get so mad at him to beat him as he did. John was a model kid. He was back in school. After school, he even started helping Larry more at the garage. He was actually being nice to his younger brothers and sisters, which was a real treat for all of us.

Life went on as usual, except dad was no longer the vibrant, strong, hardworking man he once was.

This is what my dad taught John. He did not have to listen to a woman. There were not any consequences for his actions.

Up until now, they never gave John consequences for his actions. They never set boundaries. When they did, they went overboard with their actions.

## Larry is Running the Garage

Dad started teaching Larry how to order parts to keep the business going. Larry had been doing it for quite a while as it was. He just did not want to bust dad's bubble. Larry did a fine job too; the garage business was actually starting to turn a profit.

Larry was only seventeen. Anyone knows that in a business that to make a profit you have to turn a coin over now and then. The stepmother would not let Larry pay the parts company for the parts. She wanted every cent that Larry took in. She wanted all the money, including the money from the parts. Larry had saved quite a bit of money over the years. How he did this is anyone's guess, but he did it.

Larry started dipping into his own money from his savings account, to pay for parts for all these cars. The stepmother took that money too. It just was not fair. Larry was doing his level best to keep the business afloat.

Everyone knows that the mechanic pays for the parts first. The customer pays for the parts and then some, including the labor after the repair is finished. Since Larry was using his own savings account for the parts, the money should have been his. The money collected for labor should also have been his. He was doing all the work only part of it should have gone into the household account. The stepmother did not see it that way. The stepmother being the money hungry leach that she was insisted Larry give all the money to her. She even went so far as to stay at the garage to make sure she got the money before it passed through Larry's hand

She should have been happy that she had a stepson willing and able to take over the business. We had a feeling that dad wasn't going to make it back anytime soon. Dad had never been sick a day in his life and all the customers knew dad was sick but they were willing to let Larry work on their cars. They knew he too was a good and honest mechanic.

It was around four or five months after dad's first operation. Larry had spent all of his savings ordering parts. The stepmother never gave him a dime in return to the business or to replace his savings account.

How anyone can keep the money that belongs to a son whether it be a stepson or not is beyond my comprehension. Larry had put his life's blood into helping run dads business for as long as he could remember. The whole time dad was sick Larry ran the business by himself. The customers wanted nothing to do with the woman that was our stepmother.

John's heart was not in the garage. So he didn't help Larry much. Dad bossed John around. John had to be told what to do and when. It did not come natural to him. He too was a good mechanic. He was not the enterprising person Larry was. He was not that good of a listener. He did not follow directions well.

John's first love was race car driving. Dad would not let him do it. Racing cars was John's first passion, the faster the better. He was also great with auto body repair. Dad did not want to get into that kind of a detail job. Dad should have expanded out if for no other reason he had a son willing to do it.

John was always getting into trouble racing cars at Green Gables.

Larry had to tell him every step of the way, to keep John focused.

The stepmother let Larry use up all his savings. Then she told dad they needed the garage closed. No one could run it properly.

Larry never understood why dad had let her close the garage until many, many years later, when Karen told him.

All he knew was he did his level best to make ends meet. Rightfully Larry, with John to help should have kept the garage open.

The stepmother's big ambition was to collect welfare for all of us. This was more fun to her than running an honest business.

While dad was in the hospital, he wrote Karen a letter, she was living in New Hampshire. In this letter dad wrote, "He just did not understand why Larry was stealing money from the garage. He just did not understand why Larry did not want to help out the other kids." What dad did not know was, the stepmother was lying to him.

As long as the garage was open and making a profit, the stepmother could not get welfare money for dad's kids. That is why she bleed Larry dry. She wanted to make him quit. She wanted him to fail. When she saw he was no quitter. She told dad a lie that Larry was stealing money from the garage. Larry was hurt, humiliated, and tormented over this. He could not understand why dad would think he would steal money from the garage. After all these years, he never had taken money before.

For Larry it was a blessing in disguise. Larry would have worked his fingers to the bone. Just to help each one of his younger brothers and sisters. It was bad enough for him to have done as much as he had already and losing his childhood. He did not need to lose his adulthood as well.

Larry would have kept running the garage without questioning the reasons why. Just because he did not know any better. He wanted to help those less fortunate and less able and still to this day he does.

The boys were the breadwinners and the girls were the homemakers and cooks.

What the stepmother did not know was she could have made a lot more money with the garage, than she ever got on welfare. It was an honest living. Larry would not have expected a dime. Dad did not give him money. He would never have expected it of her especially when she had his brothers and sisters to take care of.

So thank heavens she did not know these things about Larry. God took it out of Larry's hands.

If she had not made dad close up the garage in June, who knows Larry may still be supporting some of his brothers and sisters now. One thing Larry did not do and that was, he did not drink up all the profits like dad did. The customers could trust him to do a job and do it right. Dad always had a drink in his hands. Perhaps maybe Larry would have come to resent us too for having to support us for so long. Now we need never know.

In June of nineteen-hundred and sixty eight, dad had the stepmother close the garage.

Larry went to work for another business, they repaired transmissions, but he still lived at home. She got her wish she did put all of us kids on welfare. Even though she was receiving welfare checks for Larry, she made Larry give her money for room and board.

It was not too long after all this that she kicked Larry out of the house. He had graduated. He was only seventeen. Larry came home one day and she had thrown his stuff out of the window and it was on the front lawn. He was never allowed to return home again.

The step mother had the hots for Larry. But, he was not going to sully his relationship with his dad over this woman.

She was mad he would not take her to the prom with him. Larry would not be eighteen until September.

## Larry Writes an Article

When my brother Larry was a senior at West High School one of his teachers said, "Whoever gets an article published will get an 'A' for the class in journalism." Larry took the challenge. He wrote an article about our family called, "The Organized Bedlam." It was about a large family and all the problems involved in raising a large family.

At the time of publication into the Columbus Dispatch in Columbus, Ohio there were fifteen kids still living at home. In addition, my stepmother and dad who made it seventeen in all were living in the same household.

Larry wrote how large families have their own little problems. They have their own set of rules to follow and these rules are distinct for large families. I will try to recreate this article in this chapter.

Larry was the only student in his class to get an article published so he did get the 'A'.

Larry Baas

## The Organized Bedlam

Who can sleep when small children are up bouncing balls, throwing darts, jumping on their beds, skating across the wooden floor, or playing games?

That is the way it is almost every morning at the West Side home of the Baas family. The four rooms upstairs are used as bedrooms for 11 of the 14 children in our home. The three small babies and Mother and Dad have their bedrooms downstairs. Because Mother isn't upstairs with us, some of the children think they can start playing and shouting until Mother comes up, then watch out. Everything becomes quiet and all that can be heard are whispers. By then anyone who had intentions of sleeping is thoroughly awake.

My dad works (with John and me helping him) at Art's Garage, which he started in 1945 in a two-car garage behind our house. Then 15 years later, Dad moved to a three-car garage with an office and plenty of parking spaces where he still works today. For John and me, working here is more or less like attending a trade school where you get the experience for your future occupation. John feels that it keeps him busy and out of trouble.

Our family also has a dog, two cats and two canaries. Most of the time the dog chases the cats around as the cats try to get into the bird cages. One day while Mother was cooking dinner she set some pudding on top of the cabinet to cool. Lady the dog began chasing Crooked Tail, the cat. They went around and around the downstairs with the cat trying to get into a place where the dog couldn't reach him. Crooked Tail usually is safe on the cabinet, so he jumped right into the pudding. In Mother's anxiety to get the cat out of the food, several pudding dishes went to the floor. Both Lady and Crooked Tail wound up getting thrown out of the house while Mother cleaned up the mess and made more pudding.

I have read other articles about large families in which mealtime is described as being much like shifts in a factory. In our house we all get around the table together. When company comes some of us older children eat in the living room while the guests sit at the kitchen table. Once we had 18 persons sitting at the table at one time. Two of the babies sit in highchairs, which allow a little more room around the table. We have two long benches on each side of the table and two regular chairs at the ends of the table.

When we take a trip somewhere or just take an afternoon ride, we use one car- a 55 Ford station wagon. When we all pile in, four sit in the front seat: Mother, Dad, myself and the baby who sits on Mother's lap. The second seat holds four of the older children, while the third seat holds four of the smaller children. Behind the third seat we usually put anything we are carrying unless it is too big, in which case we put it on top on the car and tie it down.

Each of us has a certain job to do around the house. If that job isn't done by the time dinner is ready –no dinner. When the rest of us are through eating and if his work is finished, he gets to eat by himself. After we eat, two of the children get to wash the dishes while the rest wait to get into the tub. Most of the little ones get in in groups of two and when they are through, the older ones get in alone.

The children are not given an allowance each week, but John and I do get paid a little each week for the work we do at the garage. Half of what we earn is supposed to go into a savings. However, right now we find it more fun to spend than to save. The other children can earn money by getting A's on their report cards. For each A, he will receive a quarter. If he has tardy marks or check marks, a dime is deducted for each mark. We receive money for the collection plate at church each Sunday.

The house we live in used to be a duplex. It has four rooms and a bath upstairs and four rooms and a bath downstairs. The house has a small attic in which we store Christmas decorations, Easter baskets, etc. The house also has a small basement where Mother washes our clothes. She would like to move out of the city onto a small farm where Dad could run his business on his own property and the children could get out and run around more.

On Sunday mornings we all get up and go to Sunday school while Mother stays home and watches the baby and begins cooking Sunday dinner and Dad sleeps. After Sunday school the older children walk the smaller ones home and then go back to worship service.

Each of us children has a pin for perfect attendance for from one to seven years. There are very few times when we do not attend Sunday school or church. But sometimes someone is sick, can't find a shoe or wore his church clothes to school and got them too dirty for church.

It used to be that whenever we would go to a drive-in movie, the park or swimming, clothes always got lost, especially shoes. With so many children around, shoes are an expensive item for Dad's pocketbook. Now that everyone is older, we keep a watchful eye on clothes and shoes so they don't get lost quite as often.

There are many disadvantages as well as advantages to being part of a big family. Because you have to share with so many others, you can't have "extra" things because it would be unfair to the others. Sometimes one of the children may not receive attention when it is needed because other things have to be done.

A large family also means buying more food and clothes, higher utility bills and expenses and that there isn't always the money for going places or doing things.

But there are advantages in a large family too. There are always plenty of people around for birthday parties, playing games and talking and always someone to do something with.

Because a person never lacks company, this too can sometimes be a disadvantage when you want to be alone but younger brothers and sisters won't leave you alone. All in all, more fun can be had if we all put forth a little effort and overlook a lot of trifles.


This article was written by:
Larry A. Baas for his journalism class
and published in the Columbus Dispatch
In the magazine section on June 18, 1967
Pages 28 thru 32

## No Longer Allowed to Sing

When the stepmother came along, I could not sing in the choir at church anymore. Nor could I sing in the extra-curricular choir at school either. She said it took too much time away from home. She meant from me babysitting and taking care of things at home.

She wanted to run, play, and not stay home and take care of kids. I was ten years old what could I do.

I loved being able to sing. It made my dismal childhood livable. I was stunned. This was a lifeblood to me, lifeblood to God. I got the chance to sing through church and now I could not sing in the choir anymore. I could not believe it.

When the stepmother told me, I would be unable to go and sing any more it was devastating. I did this for me. Singing was in my blood. It kept me sane.

There was many times that if I had not been able to sing my childhood would have been worse, for me than it was.

I was not even able to do choir at school. This was not a required subject. It was an elective so the stepmother would no longer let me sing in the glee club, or the choir. There would have been after school practices. There would have been after school performances. She said, "It is no longer needed or necessary for you to do this."

The stepmother said, "You can no longer participate in any extra-curricular activities."

I said, "What do you mean I can no longer participate in extra-curricular activities. Choir is not extra-curricular." This too was devastating. I could not believe I was hearing this. This was the one subject I did well in I loved to sing.

She said, "It is an elective. It is not a required subject. You may only take those subjects that are required. It is an extra –curricular activity. Anytime you have to take time away from the home, it is extra-curricular. It takes time for the rehearsals and the concerts."

We had practices for church choir on Saturday mornings. So I was getting ready to leave. I did not think she was serious so I pretended she did not mean it and got ready to go as usual. The step-mother caught me. She said, "Where in the sam hill do you think you are going?"

I said, "I am going to Sunday school choir. I have done so every Satur-day for the past five year."

She said, "I told you, you could no longer go to choir."

I said, "Yes you did tell me no choir, I thought you meant no choir at school. I did not think you meant at church."

She said, "I meant all choirs peri-od. I meant no church choirs, not school choirs. Now get back in here and get back to your Saturday chores."

She said, "I am going out. When I return your chores better be done and the chores of all your brothers and sisters as well."

The stepmother was not usually home on Saturday's I do not know why she was home today. I knew she said the church choir. No one had stopped me before. I loved singing. To take this away from me was devastating. As many bad things as grandma and dad had done, neither one made me give up singing. No! She had not been here long before she was changing things up, for the worse.

I did not think she had meant it about church choir that I could not go. I thought no one stops a person from doing church things, do they? I hated it.

## Dad's Death and Funeral

Dad took a turn for the worse in August, and he ended up back in the hospital. The stepmother went to the hospital regularly to see dad. Dad got us to go to see him once during this whole time while he was here. The stepmother would not let us go often. He insisted we come at least once. We did not get much time because it exhausted him.

We were sure dad was dying. I think dad learned his lesson in how hard we took our mother's death. He wanted to make sure we knew every step of the way what was going on with him.

Dad wanted every one of us kids to come up to his room to see him. The hospital would not allow it. A child had to be at least sixteen to be able to go up to the hospital room. They were sticklers for the rules back then, no kids allowed. I was the only one who went up to our dad's room to see him I was sixteen years old.

Even though dad was dying, the younger ones could not go up to his room to see him. I only went once. I had a babysitting job and I babysat outside of the home to earn extra money. There were those days that dad insisted that we all go to see him, he stood at the window of his hospital room and waved to us. He could not stay there for long though it wore him out.

This August was one of those months where the days were hot the whole month through or so it seemed to us. Here we were out on the blacktop parking lot in a hot car (air conditioned cars had not been invented yet, not that we would have been allowed to used it). The stepmother made us stay in the car. We were not allowed to open windows or doors; she did not want the authorities knowing she kept twelve kids in a car on a hot day. It was too hot. I did not understand the purpose of making us stay in the hot car during the summer, the hottest month of the year. It just did not make any sense to me. I was afraid to let them out of the car. I would have gotten a beaten if I did not follow the stepmother's orders implicitly.

We did open up windows and doors. This would have upset her than we could easily roll them back up and as soon as she left, we would roll them back down again.

There was not any water. We could not go to the bathroom. Boys could go to the back lot girls could not. Oh! How I hated coming here. I had babysat before what is the big deal now. We could not go up and see him.

Dad died in August of 1968. He was no longer in pain.

It was a mess too as usual. The only person who was with dad was the stepmother. Usually they call the family in when the time is close they did not do this with dad.

Junior called Vera and said, "Your dad just died."

Five minutes later Junior called Vera and said, "Your dad is dying aren't you going to go and visit him before he dies." Is he dead or not? I thought this was mean of everyone that was involved in this fiasco. It was a cruel joke. Everyone knows Vera was never dad's favorite. They argued as much as dad and grandma did. (Grandma Baas and the stepmother did the same thing to Vera as Junior had done. They called her up and said, "Your dad just died." Then they called up and said, "When are you going to visit your dad in the hospital.")Vera was really upset about it. She did not know what to believe by this time. Was her dad truly dead? What kind of a family would do these things to a person? Dayton was not that close. She did not have a driver's license.

Neither Junior nor anyone else offered to take Vera to Dayton so that she could see our dad. With her not having a license it made it difficult for her to go by herself.

The funeral and the obituary were not very friendly either.

Oh! The stepmother said all the right things and did all the right things but she refused to have my dad buried by my mother. Even when our mother died, our parents bought two plots. My parents had been married for nineteen years. The stepmother refused to let dad be buried beside our mother. Even after all this time and my mother dead and now my dad was dead; my mother was still a threat to the stepmother.

In the obituary, the stepmother refused to let Vera and John's names be mentioned. Their names were purposely missing from my dad's (their dad's) obituary. She mentioned all six of her kids. Five of her kids were not even my dad's children. No matter what your children do you still want to acknowledge them!

No one seemed to care what happened to us now.

I did not understand what was happening. Our stepmother was no relation to us. Why do we have to stay here? There is no one to protect us from this woman. Is it ok for us to stay here with a woman who does not even like us? It just did not make any sense to me. She is not our mom. She does not want to be out mom. She never did. She loved the power it brought, the notoriety. People would see her and say what a wonderful thing she is doing giving these children a mother. I think she thought we did not hear, but we heard. She is so young too.

Why was grandma Baas not jumping in to take us away from this horrible mean person? She tried to take us from our dad when our mother died. Now she just did not care. She thought we were only getting what we deserve.

Oh! How I hated them all now! I do not usually use this word but I did now. I hated 514 South Harris Avenue and everything it represented.

Many years after my dad died my stepmother moved to Florida. She had her oldest son buried in the plot next to my dad.

## Locked In the Basement

It is the summer of nineteen hundred and sixty nine. Dad has been dead a year now or almost a year. I am working for Lazarus Department Stores and Jimmy has a paper-route. Jimmy and I are bringing in some extra money. Larry and John joined the Air Force; it was either that or be drafted into the Army. The Army was a sure sign of seeing combat in Viet-Nam. They opted for the lesser of two evils. Vera had joined the Air Force a year ago.

This summer starts like any other summer. The stepmother is gone a lot during the day never says where she is going, just leaves. She does not come back until bedtime. Debbie is now stuck watching the kids. She is also earning money. She is also babysitting other people's kids. She loves it. The kids love her. The kids are all pretty well running wild in the house, no organizing of any sort. Course there is still this thing about cleaning and keeping it clean or else, a beating. It was kept clean.

Debbie is now the chief cook, because by the time I get off work it is too late to cook. Fun! Fun! Fun! I do have fun too. No one at work can believe what is going on of course I do not tell them anything bad just how many children there are, safe topics. We were taught to not tell about anything that happened at home. But they find it hard to believe twelve children still live at home.

The stepmother cannot stand Debbie's cooking. She feels Debbie is not very creative, always cooking spaghetti with bacon. Yuck! For spaghetti with bacon, instead of using hamburger. Double yuck! And that is putting it mildly. She is fifteen years old, with the household responsibility, course Joan is her back-up support a long with, Jimmy. Still, it's too much responsibility for one so young I know I have been there. For her you never knew when an attack of the fits would seize hold of her. She did manage to keep it under control most of the time.

All year long the stepmother would lock us in the basement. When she wanted rid of us for a day or two. One time we were locked in for a whole week. We were without food. We were without water, just each other for company. She started threatening placement into an orphanage somewhere but never she elaborated where. I told my boss and even turned in my notice. The stepmother was pissed off now. She did not have extra money coming in from my job. The kids were watching or looking up to me now for guidance and she hated that even more.

We did get smarter though. We started hiding plates; silverware, can openers, drinking glasses, and anything that you can think of to not go hungry or thirsty.

You see all the canned goods were stored in the basement.

Every kind of canned good imagi-nable, we did not get to cook this food. We made sure we ate only those things that did not need cooking. We ate canned peaches, canned pears, applesauce, canned corn and green beans. They were not too bad either. Spaghettio's had been popular and beef ravioli, we learned to like these cold. When you are hungry, you do not care what you had to eat. We were hungry. I cannot tell you how many days, weeks, or even months we were locked up down in the basement. I remember there were several days in a row we were locked down in the basement with nothing to eat. That is why we started hiding can openers, silverware, and plates in the basement. We called it our emergency stash. We never knew when a mood would strike our stepmother and we would be locked in the basement. It was only my dad's kids, who were locked down in the basement. Her kids did not get the same treatment.

Oh! Sometimes we got a real treat we made homemade icing. Just water, powdered milk and sugar but we were in seventh heaven. Sometimes we even used vanilla which was a very rare treat. I was so good. No! It was delicious.

When the stepmother found out we had been eating her stashes of food, she forced us to eat off the floor. When we were locked in the basement, we ate food (the canned goods) that was supposed to be eaten at the dinner table. This food was supposed to feed us all. It was not just for those of us who were locked in the basement we had no right to do these things.

As far as I am concerned, she had no right to lock us in the basement. She especially did not have any rights to keep us from eating. I do not remember any of us being overweight.

To this day, we are all afraid of basements and small spaces. At night it is especially gruesome. I cannot go out to my car and make sure it is locked. If I need something out of my car my poor husband has to go and get it for me. I just cannot do it.

Thank you God for giving me such a patient husband!

Do not even lock us in the basement as a joke. It is not a joke.

## Eating off the Floor

The stepmother threatened many times to make us eat off the floor. We always thought she was doing it in jest. She was not kidding. Eventually she was successful in pulling off the threat.

There were many things leading up to us eating off the floor. The main thing was being locked in the basement and eating her stored food items. What were we to do? We were hungry!

Another reason for eating off the floor was the breaking of too many plates. You get tense and it slips out of your hands. You get in a hurry scraping plates and the dishes drop out of your hands. The silverware accidently goes into the wastebasket. As a kid, you do not see it; after all it is not your money that bought it.

The night we forgot to clean (sweep) the floor after dinner. So finally, the stepmother is fed up, she said, "You want to eat like animals, well I will see to it that you do."

While we were in school one day, she had the table removed. Tonight she cooked. This was a rare occasion. We had potatoes (mashed), gravy, unsliced roast beef, and corn, with no silverware and no plates. Nothing to cut the meat with, just our hands, maybe our hands were washed maybe they weren't. Who cared! We sat on the floor Indian style; the food was served in large communal bowls. For the longest time she just stood over us with the bull whip in her hand. We just looked at the food.

She said, "Eat." We all just stared at this food for a long time. She is handling the bull whip threatening to use it if we did not get busy eating. She is shaking this thing the whole time while standing over us. Very intimidating!

Still no one moved. Then she kicked me in the back. It hurt badly. As hard as she could muster, she kicked me in the back again. Degradation, humiliation is not even, close to how you feel at a time like this. You look at this community bowl (pot) actually. She expected us to dive in and eat, virtually like animals. I could not believe my eyes.

I decided, immediately she wanted to see an animal eat, well she ain't seen an animal eat till I show her. Yes! I was going to put on a show. I was mad. God gave me the guts to do this just once! He told me if you want to make yourself and your brothers and sisters feel better at the same time you go right ahead. God does not want us to be defiant. Sometimes we have to be. For me the time was now, when one is trying to degrade you. If I am wrong than I am sorry but for this moment in time, I was defiant. The stepmother hated this side of me too. A person can only take so much. I was at my wits end.

I grabbed the mashed potatoes. I got the biggest handful my hand could take. I shoved it all into my mouth at once. I had it smeared all over myself, by the time I was done. The other kids thought it was great. They started laughing. I had at least broken the tension. Some of them followed suit. I wasn't done though; I took the gallon milk jug and turned it completely upside down. It went everywhere except in my mouth. This milk was all over my face, in my eyes, in my hair, and all down the front of my shirt. I wanted to make it into a joke. Which was my intent it made me sick, to even consider it. Can you imagine the thought process of looking at these mashed potatoes, gravy, corn, uncut roast beef, no silverware, and no knife to cut the meat? No plates nothing to dig into the pot, to eat the food with, just your fingers and hands. What do you do with this? The stepmother did not like that one bit. I had out foxed her.

She grabbed me by the hair of my head, stood me up, and took her fist and put it into my jaw. Ouch! It hurt. It left a bruise and her fist print. Still I felt proud of myself, for not letting her get the best of the situation.

I took a bad situation and made it grand. That was God's intent. I had to do something or we would have been lost forever emotionally. God knew this.

Thank you God for giving me the courage and the wit to stand up to these abusers, they could not affect our minds and make us criminals. You were not going to allow that. Thank you God! I cannot give you enough praise for this moment and for this memory of keeping me sane.

Heck, a kid can only take so much. Then they start fighting back. If they do not start fighting back, they take it out on themselves later. I was tired of beating myself up for something I did not do or cause. Worst case scenario they may take it out on another kid later in life.

Yes! We all make mistakes but the punishments never fit the crime in our house. It always seemed to me that the adults in our house were the ones going berserk. They were the ones going off the deep end.

We had a saying when we were kids our parents must stay awake all night long to think of newer and more bazar ways to punish us. It just did not make any sense.

It did not get any easier.

## The Last Christmas on Harris Ave.

I turned sixteen the year dad died.

Lazarus Department Store loved to help the community. They were going to hire all of us kids who were sixteen years old and older. John and Larry were gone already. Karen had left a few years ago. I was the only one that was old enough. I got a job working as a dishwasher at the Highlander Grill in the west basement. For me it was the best. I loved it. Two other kids worked here with me too. We got along great. These two teenage kids like me were working. I think they felt sorry for me.

Lazarus did not stop helping us out here though. Every chance they got they helped us out some more.

My dad's Christmas train was abandoned years ago. The stepmother hated it. She hated it because it represented our mother. Lazarus would not have known about the tin train though.

One week before Christmas, they wanted to do some more things for us. They were that kind of a store. They were always helping the community wherever they saw the need.

What they did for us this Christmas was impressive. They gave us three truckloads of stuff. It seemed like they just would not quit bringing the stuff in. The items kept coming and coming with armloads of stuff for us. The people bringing them in just would not quit.

They brought us a Christmas tree with all the trimmings. The Christmas tree was beautiful. It had many beautiful lights. It had garland, tinsel, and ornaments. It was not dad's tree but it was still beautiful. The stepmother did not like Christmas. We probably would not have had a tree this year if it were not for the help of Lazarus. It was a beautiful Christmas tree.

It was one of the most beautiful Christmas trees, I had ever seen.

There were soups and canned goods of all kinds. It took a lot to feed a family this size. They must have given us a week's supply of groceries; maybe a month's supply maybe a year's supply that is how much it appeared to be to me. There was bread. There was cold cereal, which we usually never have to eat, too expensive for a family this size.

One week before Christmas, they brought all this stuff.

Now if that was not enough bringing us all this food, they also brought presents. There were more presents than you could imagine.

There were still twelve of us at home. There were shopping bags full of clothes. Each bag had a kids name on it. There were shopping bags full of toys. Each bag of toys had a kids name on it. There must have been age appropriate toys inside each bag. It was neat. For one week, we looked at all this stuff. We tried snooping around to see what all we were getting. We did not want to disturb anything. We were afraid of being caught snooping. It was exciting.

I remember now my boss and all my associates quizzing me for names and ages of all the kids in the family. I did not think anything of it at the time. Just thought they liked me and wanted to know about me and my family. We kept wondering how did these people who sent packages knew our names and ages. This must have been how they got all the names right on the packages.

We had never seen so much good food. Hams were expensive and we did not get them very often. The ham put into a pot of bean soup, was the only time we got ham. Then it was ham hocks, not quite as good as a ham. Ham hocks made some of the best bean soup though.

All of us were excited. As Christmas day got closer, the more excited we became.

The big day is finally here.

We wake up. We creep down the stairs quiet as a mouse. We avoided all the squeaky steps. We did not want to wake up the stepmother and get her mad. No not today! We did not want to make her mad!

When we got in the living room, we could not believe what we were seeing. Everything was gone. The Christmas tree was gone. All the presents with our names on them were gone. We just could not believe it. The hams, turkeys, and food all gone, it had disappeared.

The kids in the house were slowly started coming down the steps. They all started crying. They were hysterical. Yes! Us older ones were crying too not visibly, we were crying the no shed tears kind of a cry. We never got anything remotely close to what we had been seeing all week.

There was a note. Santa had left a note. He took everything lock, stock, and barrel. It read that since we were so bad this year Santa decided to take all of our presents away from us this year instead of leaving us presents. The kids were all crying and upset. I too was upset not because I did not get a present but because all the kids were upset. Sure, I was a kid and wanted to cry too. To say otherwise would be a lie. I did not cry because that would have made it worse.

We could not find the stepmother anywhere. She had disappeared. I had to deal with this mess, all the crying. I was sixteen and there were twelve of us still at home. There were the six of us and six of the stepmother's kids and one of them being our half-brother. The youngest of these kids was three years old.

It was bad enough that I had to console all these kids by myself. We could not find the stepmother anywhere. She just left. She did not leave a note.

We only had Santa's note.

When I got back to work at the Highlander Grill at Lazarus my boss asked me how was my Christmas.

You see we did not know it was Lazarus Department Stores, who had sent all these presents to us, until my boss spilt the beans. I told my boss, "Christmas was great. We had so much stuff it was unbelievable." I never told my boss, that Santa had taken everything lock, stock and barrel. It was a terrible time.

## Jimmy Goes To Franklin Village

I told you earlier I worked at Lazarus. Before this, I had a lot of babysitting jobs. With this money, I used some for transportation. The rest I put it into a savings account. I had to give some to the stepmother for room and board. I was sixteen years old. I paid for my own dental bills and glasses. I made eighty-five cents an hour at Lazarus.

Jimmy also had a job. His job was a paper route. He carried the dispatch for several years. He was very good at what he did. His customers like him a lot. He got many tips. He put most of his into a savings account. We both had a lot saved. Jimmy was twelve years old.

After several years of having these accounts open, our stepmother closed them both and spent the money. You could not collect welfare if anyone had savings accounts, so she had to close them.

Jimmy had a big blow-up with her. She started buying things like a new T.V., a couch and a few other things. In the meantime, his bank account was empty of all his money. He came home from collecting his paper-route money and turned on the T.V.

The stepmother said, "What in the sam hill do you think you are doing?"

He said, "I am watching my T.V. set!"

She said, "What makes you think it is your T.V. set!"

Jimmy said, "Well you paid for it with my money, out of my savings account."

She said, "I did not." She turned off the set. Jimmy turned on the T.V. set. She turned it off again. He turned it on. With that, she smacked Jimmy as hard as she could across the face. He hit her back. She hit him again. He hit her. This time she was mad. She took the belt to him.

She dragged him out of the house and pushed him into the car. She was beating him with the belt the whole way to the car.

She took him to Franklin County Children's Services to have him committed into Franklin Village for unruly children.

The caseworker there had a talk with Jimmy. She told the stepmother that she could find no grounds with which to keep him. The caseworker said, "They needed to work out their differences at home." The woman said, "Is there no other relative who could or would want to take this child in for a time being."

The stepmother was even madder it made her look like an idiot.

The caseworker could find nothing wrong with Jimmy. She said, "She did not find Jimmy un-cooperative." This made her even madder. Madder than even Jimmy had seen her, but after a while a kid can only take so much then you have to start fighting back. Jimmy was up to his limits. Taking his hard earned money was the last draw. I am sure that it helped Jimmy to know he had gotten her mad.

She took him to Grandma Baas' house. He was there about twelve hours before Grandma Baas had, had enough. Grandma Baas wanted Jimmy to apologize to his mother, (not his stepmother, but his mother) and he refused to do so. She made him leave her house as well and wanted nothing more to do with him.

They shipped him off to one of his Aunt's house. So all summer long Jimmy was at the Aunts house. They treated him like royalty. He was permitted to see the side of life that allows you to have many nice things if you have a lot of money.

If the stepmother would have taken him to Grandma Lamb's house it would have been a different story. Grandma Lamb would have taken Jimmy into her house in a heartbeat.

Time goes on and still Jimmy does not come home. We did not even know where he had gone or with whom. One day the stepmother came home and said, "Norma J-e-a-n, (when she says your whole name you know you are in trouble), Norma J-e-a-n." She marches her ass right up the steps and flips on the light. I am sound asleep. Everyone else is sound asleep too. Not for long though. It is very startling to be awakened in such a loud obnoxious manner.

The stepmother said, "Why did you tell Grandma Lamb Jimmy was in Franklin Village?" Smack, Smack.

I said, "He is?" "Boo! Hoo! Hoo! Hoo!" I could not believe my ears; my little brother was in Franklin Village. This is where they send bad kids! We were in trouble. "How did he get there?"

The stepmother said, "I put him there and you told Grandma Lamb."

I said, "I did not. I had no idea he was there. Boo! Hoo! Hoo!" I was sobbing like a banshee. I was sobbing so bad I had drool coming out of my mouth. I must have been a sight.

The stepmother said, "You were the only one with access to a phone."

You would have thought since I was having such a strong reaction she could have figured it out that I had no idea he was even in Franklin Village. But she didn't have a clue. It was always about her and what she wanted. She was never looking to see how other people react to how she acts.

I said, "I didn't do it. I had no idea Boo! Hoo!"

I found out years later my oldest brother Junior had told Grandma Lamb and she was pissed off. You did not want to mess with Grandma. We did not know until years later that he had been at Aunt Frieda's the whole summer.

## Sneaking Out

Now there comes a time when all hell breaks loose. We have been sneaking out of the house for months, maybe even years. If you cannot play outside during the day, you will sneak out to play at night. That is the nature of the kids. I did not do it very often but I have been known to do it on occasion.

One day Joan, Debbie, and Fred snuck out. They were slick as a whistle too. I would have never known they were that sneaky. Once outside they went in two different locations. Probably a good thing as it turns out. This one time in particular they did it and just as Joan was sneaking in the window next door, someone broke a gallon jug of milk. You could hear the noise for what seemed like blocks around, it was so loud. It was summertime and all the windows everywhere were open. There were no air conditioning units.

The stepmother too heard the noise. She was sitting out on our front porch. She turned her head to see what was going on. What she sees really surprises her. She sees Joan climbing into the window next door. She hollers, "Joan! What in the hell do you think you are doing?" She grabbed a switch off the tree and pulled Joan back out the window by the hair on her head. Just that quick! I would have never believed she could move so fast. I was peeking out of the downstairs bedroom window. The step-mother whipped Joan all the way home. Then she proceeded to turn on all the lights in the house to find out who else was missing, if anyone. Yep! Sure enough, Debbie and Fred were also missing. Joan got a beating. The step-mother gave me a beating as well.

She said, "Norma you let them sneak outside."

I said, "No I did not, I did not see them." If I had, I would have tried to talk them out of it. I felt it was too early. It was still daylight. Usually they snuck out at night. They were getting bolder with this move. I would not have stopped them either, nor would I have squealed either. They knew I would have tried to talk them out of it that is why they did not let me know.

The stepmother said, "You are a liar."

I said, "No, I'm not lying, I did not see them nor did I allow them. They snuck out when I was not looking."

Now I got another beating for lying. I also get a beating for letting them sneak out in the first place. I did not know they had snuck out. The stepmother did not believe me. Since I let them sneak out I got another whipping. Just because I was the oldest, I should have stopped them from sneaking out.

Joan spoke up and said, "Norma did not know."

The stepmother told Joan to stay out of it or she (meaning me) would get some more. I got more of a beating. It did not bother me. What bothered me was Joan was getting a beating also, for sneaking out.

Fred and Debbie were in a world of trouble with, a capital "T". They managed to sneak back in the house without the stepmother's knowledge. I told Debbie and Fred to sneak back out and not look back. They did exactly that they did sneak back out. Joan and I told them both we could not stand for another brother or sister to get another beating. Freddie backed out the window. Debbie backed out the window, without the stepmother ever knowing they had ever come back into the house (they were slick).

Debbie and Freddie were separated from each other, now though. Debbie thought Freddie was following close behind. The next thing she knew Fred had disappeared. She hollered for him a couple of times, no answer. Freddie was more afraid of not knowing, where to go or what to do he lagged behind. Debbie had to look out for herself now or get a beating. She like us was tired of getting beatings.

The stepmother had called in reinforcements. Junior and Grandma Lamb came to help search for Debbie but she hid well.

I do not know why she thought Debbie would come out for Junior and grandma. Neither one of them had proven to be trustworthy. Now would not be any different. We had lived with grandma, sometimes she was ok but not always. We knew what we were getting into here.

You see the bullwhip was Junior's idea. He thought it would be neat to make a strap instead of using a belt. It was his idea to take a car hose, slice it into four strips all the way down to make a handle. This left a grip to hold onto. Take this and beat the kids with it. This way you use less of your own strength and get four hits with one.

No one was going to find her hidden in the tall grasses of the neighbor's yard. She had tried to get one of the neighborhood kids to help her to hide. He told his parents. Their parents told the stepmother, Debbie sensing something wrong, hides in a different place. She stays hidden all night long. She does not go home. The next morning Debbie went to Grandma Lamb's house. This was a safe haven from the stepmother at least. The stepmother was mad. She was madder than any of us had seen her before.

We had to go out and look for Debbie too. We would never have turned Debbie in. The stepmother did not know that. We did not want to see her get a beating.

We think the stepmother was hoping they would expose themselves to us. Freddie did not stay hidden. He got a really hard and bad beating. It sickened me even more to have to watch and be able to do nothing.

Dad at least had moments when he was fun. Grandma Lamb too was fun sometimes. I do not remember the step-mother ever being fun as a child.

The stepmother never tried to see if there might be a better way of handling things. Always ready to give us beating first, last, and always. No matter what we did.

We had been planning for quite a while to leave. This only reinforced what we had been planning.

Our plans were that as soon as I turned eighteen, get an apartment, and move every one of my brothers and sisters in with me. I would be eighteen next year. I already had a job. As I left every one of my brothers and sisters were going to leave with me. I was not going to leave without them. We were leaving lock stock and barrel. We did not think about whether we had enough money to live on. We already knew how to cook, clean, pay bills. What more did one need to learn to have a life free of beatings, free of stress?

We felt like we needed to wait until one of us was of legal age before we could go. I was going to be the first to reach the legal age of eighteen. I will have graduated and gotten a diploma.

Beyond this we did not think. I just knew I could not leave my brothers and sisters in this hell whole. They all loved the idea.

We were afraid that if we did not leave we were going to kill the woman who is our stepmother. We thought if we did this, we would all be in prison. We were scared we had never planned anything so daring. We knew it was the best thing for us.

What we didn't know or had forgotten you could hear everything through the vents downstairs from the front bedroom. So the stepmother knew what we were planning every step of the way.

The stepmother had already kicked Larry out as soon as he graduated. She had already gotten rid of John. She made Karen run away. She also kicked Vera and Junior out. Course she kicked them out before she ever moved into our house.

We started saving money to be prepared for such an emergency.

Now with Debbie gone to who knows where. She never came home that night. Jimmy was living with one of our aunts and uncles. He had been there all summer long.

What is going to happen to the rest of us? There are still four of us left in the stepmother's house. What will they do to us now?

# Epilog

These are my childhood memories.

I have attempted to bring them back to life to the best of my abilities. There were many more stories I could have told. These are just a small sampling of our lives living with an abusive step-mother and an alcoholic father.

As in my previous two books, I hope this book helps those families in need of help.

If you see yourself in any of these situations please seek help. Get family counseling. If you are a parent, please stop the abuse. Your child only wants you to love them. They in turn will love you.

If you are a child, please seek help from a trusted friend or adviser. Seek help from your teacher.

If you are a child, none of this is your fault. Do not take the blame it is not your fault. Do not let your parents blame you.

If you are a teacher or a person in authority, please watch for these signs of abuse. Help those children who are in your care.

However, tread carefully for the child's sake. Always keep in mind the punishment a child may receive for letting the secret out.

Remember with God, all things are possible. The abuse can stop. One has to actively work to stop the abuse and raise mentally healthy children.


Do not give up.
Continue to be strong.
God will help you with every step.
You can stop!
Do it now, before it is too late!

Twenty years ago, one of my younger sisters and I went to a garage sale on Harris Avenue. This sale was run by the lady who had purchased 514. We asked her what had happened to the house at 514. She said, "I had it torn down because of all the children's screams we could hear from it all day and all night long. No one could live there. The house was haunted."

This freaked us out because we were those children. It seems we had left a part of us in the house.

She said, "The neighbors came from all around and cheered as the house was demolished because they too had heard the screams."

I ended book three with the kids sneaking out at night. Debbie running away and not coming back now what will become of us? The whole house is out of control. The stepmother's kids are not here. She sent them away.

What will become of us now?
Will we be punished?
Will we be put into an institution?
Will we be separated forever?
Will we stay with the step mother?

Look for Book 4 of
**The Tin Train Series**

# 'The Home'

It will be out in the **spring of 2014**

5696905R30114

Made in the USA
San Bernardino, CA
17 November 2013